HOURS *of* TORTURE
YEARS *of* SILENCE

My Soul was the Scene of the Crime

Teresa Lauer, M.A.

Institute for Interpersonal Relations
Pacific Grove, California

Published by:

Institute for Interpersonal Relations

612 Lighthouse Ave., Suite 238

Pacific Grove, CA 93950

408-658-0196

e-mail: iirelate@ix.netcom.com

Printed in the United States of America

ISBN 0-9662078-0-7

Lauer, Teresa.
    Hours of torture, years of silence : my soul was the scene
of the crime / Teresa Lauer. -- 1st ed.
1. Lauer, Teresa. 2. Rape victims--Biography. 3. Rape trauma syndrome.
I. Title

RC560.R36L38 1998   362.883'092
                           QB198-3

This book is dedicated to my husband, Phil.

Each life is blessed with graces,
and I have been privileged
beyond my expectations,
beyond my dreams,
in my life with you.

Acknowledgments

This book exists because of the people in my life. Their love and encouragement, their support, their acceptance of me, and particularly the intimate moments we've shared, mean more to me than they will ever know.

First, I am forever indebted to my husband, Phil. You saved my life and gave me a reason to live. These are such small words, undeserving of the part you played in my being alive. This is not said for folly or dramatics, but is my truth. Thank you for your honesty and sense of humor, so sorely needed while writing this book. Thank you for the energy and courage you gave freely each time I asked. And thank you for your unconditional love and for helping me realize that I matter.

Next, I'd like to thank my mom, Lillian, for her acceptance of me after learning of the unacceptable and unimaginable. Mom, I can't thank you enough for being you, for loving me as you always have, and for giving me the freedom to become the person I am today.

I'd like to thank my closest friend, Sally Lucido. Sally, how can I thank you for your belief in me? You are the Ethel to my Lucy. No dream was ever discouraged or laughed at, but rather encouraged with a love and friendship that's rare. For that, I thank you from the bottom of my heart. You'll be my sister, always.

I'd also like to thank Dr. Dennis Hinkle, a very treasured friend. Dennis, thank you for your friendship and your honesty. You live life fully and encourage me to do the same. Thank you for giving your time and knowledge so unselfishly, and for helping me believe in myself. You convinced me that I can make a difference, for which I'm eternally grateful.

Special thanks to my psychologist, Dr. Gary Bushweiler. Gary, it's difficult for me to understand the intimacy and intensity of our relationship, but I'm a better person because of it. You helped unearth fragile feelings and coax long-overdue tears. You inspired me to find the courage to explore my inner world. You will be in my heart, always.

Thanks also to my editor, Bill Greenleaf. Bill, your honest (interactive!) critique and editing skills have made my manuscript, and the finished product, something of which I can be truly proud. Your kind attention helped me communicate my decidedly difficult thoughts and feelings. Thank you.

Introduction

My client sat before me, her pain palpable. Only glimpses of her soft, gray eyes were visible as she sat with her chin nearly touching her chest. She was young, 22, and petite, with long, dark hair and I'd grown to like her very much, though we'd only had four sessions together. Dressed in jeans and a sweatshirt, she pressed herself deeper into my couch.

"I was, well . . . you know, raped . . . a couple of years ago," she stammered, " . . . and, I . . . I can't seem to . . . I'm falling apart." She looked deep in my eyes now, pleading for help.

This was, she went on to tell me, the first time she'd told anyone what happened to her. A tear rolled down her cheek as she lowered her head once again.

I let her words rest in the air, and was grateful for the silence. My office was bathed in quiet; even the noises from the street below faded to the background. The walls, painted a soft apricot and the couch, a slightly darker hue of the same color, seemed to enfold her. The only lamp in the room cast a soft glow on her face and I was suddenly aware of how dark it had become outside.

Turning from her, I reached for a reference book on sexual assault on the shelf over my desk, and wiped away a tear that had rolled down *my* cheek. Information she had supplied earlier suddenly made sense with her new revelation.

In quickly putting together parts of her history and this new account, I suspected she had PTSD, post-traumatic stress disorder. Further information would be helpful, and I needed to educate her on the symptoms so that she would realize that she wasn't going crazy and that her feelings and behaviors were a normal response to an abnormal event. At that point, we could talk about a therapy plan.

I moved my chair closer to the couch where she sat and opened the book. We read the criteria together.

The first set of symptoms in meeting a diagnosis of post-traumatic stress disorder address exposure to a traumatic event. Exposure in this case, relates to having witnessed or been confronted with an event, either natural (such as a flood or hurricane) or man-made (such as rape, war, physical or sexual assault), in which one was actually injured or threatened with injury or death. The traumatic events cause the victim to experience an intense response such as tremendous fear, terror, or helplessness. The event could have occured at any time in the past. My client clearly met this criteria.

"Yes," she said, looking up from the book at me. "Yes . . . that's me. It was awful. I'd known him for years. I trusted him, but . . . I thought he was going to hurt me if I didn't do what he wanted." She looked back down at the page.

The next set of symptoms address the persistent re-experiencing of the trauma, including nightmares, flashbacks, insomnia, intrusive thoughts of the trauma, becoming panicky and shaky when thinking of the trauma, and becoming upset around the anniversary of the event. Understandably, re-experiencing is often terribly confusing and distressing.

Flashbacks, in particular, can terrify a trauma victim. They strike suddenly and are extremely emotional events in themselves. One doesn't black out but there is a feeling of having left oneself temporarily, causing a sort of numbing effect. Flashbacks can be so vivid that one can smell or see or feel the event happening to them again. Each individual experiences different triggers for these flashbacks and other forms of re-experiencing, however, these symptoms are most likely to convince one of the need for help.

"I keep seeing his face in front of me, when I close my eyes . . . when I'm awake . . . it doesn't seem to matter. All I see is him. And the dreams lately, I don't understand why I keep dreaming about him." She looked at me for an answer but brought her eyes back to the page; she wanted to have the full picture of what she was experiencing.

The re-experiencing of feelings such as fear, shame, and guilt, among others, leads to avoidance of the pain of re-experiencing the trauma and, as a result, leads to a greater need for help. Avoidance can take many forms such as not wanting to talk or think about the trauma and avoiding certain places or activities in order not to be reminded of the trauma. A client once displayed an example of avoidance of her feelings each time she saw a man wearing a sweatshirt bearing the name of the college she attended years prior. While living in a dorm on campus, she was physically assaulted in her room. She was rescued before a sexual assault could occur, but was convinced that she could be have been seriously injured or killed that night. The only thing she remembered seeing of her attacker was the name of the school on his sweatshirt. She left college soon after, but continued to feel "numb" each time she saw a sweatshirt such as the one he wore.

This set of criteria was harder for her to evaluate, so we looked at different areas of her life. How had school been going? Was she still involved in the track team? Was she dating? How did she feel about her part-time job? Did she go out with friends often?

"No," she replied to my last question. "I don't go out anymore with anyone really. I used to like to go shopping and stuff with friends, but now I just figure, what's the use? It seems like I don't really have that much in common with them. They're excited about their plans and dreams, and . . . I just feel like I don't have goals anymore; in fact, my grades have slipped a little lately," she added, with slight embarrassment. I asked how that fit into what she'd just read.

"Well," she said, looking at me. "I . . . I thought maybe . . . I didn't know what was happening, but here it is right here. Maybe this has something to do with how I've been feeling lately . . . just not interested in anything any more."

She sat fingering the pages of the book, reading the criteria over and over. I could sense that she was determining how this information pertained to her, and urged her to continue.

My client had identified with several of the aspects of PTSD, however when reading the fourth set of symptoms regarding increased arousal, she seemed unable to relate to any of them, such as becoming irritable and angry, being unable to fall asleep or sleeping too much, or becoming overly concerned with her safety. Of the symptoms she had displayed, these were by far the least identifiable to her.

I helped her with the last set of criteria. I'd noticed that she'd jumped when

I called her from the waiting room; an exaggerated startle response. And, I reminded her, she'd mentioned that she was extremely angry driving lately. She had this rage, she said, that she felt barely able to contain. I gave her an assignment for the following week: to try and determine how many of the other symptoms of this section she noticed. She returned to the last two items.

I suspected that my client was suffering from a mild form of PTSD. Thankfully, she had come for help early and, based on her answers to the two remaining criteria - duration and the disturbance to her overall functioning - was not yet suffering from long-term or severe PTSD.

"Yes. Yes," she said nodding. "This has been going on for what seems forever. But, well, it's been only about four months and . . . it's what I really came to see you about." She lowered her head.

She identified several of the symptoms that were particularly difficult for her; those she wanted to work on first. Our time was up, too soon. I knew that she was a voracious reader and recommended several very good books she could read before our next appointment. She had much to think about, as did I.

I looked around my office after my last client left that evening. It was dark now, and only the small lamp cast a soft glow around the room. I thought about my client who'd revealed the fact that she'd been raped. She'd taken an important first step, and I was pleased that she was finding her voice. Her journey was just beginning, and while I knew my purpose was to help her find her own understanding of what had happened to her, I wondered what I might have told her of my own experience . . .

I'd tell her that it wasn't her fault. Not then. Not now. Not ever.

I'd tell her that there's a spectrum of emotions that occur during her hour with me, but that their meaning is often assigned elsewhere.

I'd tell her no matter what she wore, no matter what she said, no matter how she acted, she didn't deserve to be raped.

I'd tell her that the nightmares, when she can sleep, *do* go away . . . eventually. And that they may come back when she least expects it.

I'd resist the urge to present my own three years of therapy as if they made any sense to me at the time, because they didn't. There are ragged edges, muted lines, and confusion.

I'd tell her that the raw, vulnerable emotions that feel so overwhelming when alone and contemplative, will feel less so when she's able to share them with someone.

I'd tell her that it's extremely difficult to accept the unacceptable, and that resistance is exhausting.

The work of therapy for post-traumatic stress disorder, I'd tell her, is intense, but crucial. And, I would tell her, it may get worse before it gets better.

I'd tell her that she will experience intimacy and love in her life again, perhaps where she least expects it.

Guilt and shame may be emotions she'll experience as most rape victims do, I'd tell her, but don't invest in them. They won't serve any purpose whatsoever.

I'd tell her that she will begin to let people into her heart again . . . in her own time. Acceptance, I'd tell her, will come . . . again, in her own time. And taking the time she needs, is okay.

But most importantly . . . I'd tell her she's not alone.

I sat thinking, in the soft glow of the light, of my own journey . . .

Chapter 1

November, 1994

The first time it happened, well, I wasn't certain *what* it was. I was just . . . shopping. That's the last thing I remember, anyway. It was a little more than a week before Thanksgiving, and the mall was humming with excitement. Being a Tuesday, most of the other shoppers were young moms with their kids. Red and green glimmering tinsel wound its way around the upper level rails and flowed over, raining on the Santa and elves and playing children below. Along with the music, that's the most wonderful sound of the holidays . . . children playing. Somehow, though, it seemed a little sad that day.

I was running late, but thought I'd make one more stop at Nordstrom, my last before going home. The display in the window of the gourmet candy store next door was enchanting. Gold foil packages of luscious chocolate candies woven between red and green silk strands invited me in, but my eyes went past the window to a rack of silk blouses right inside the entrance to Nordstrom. They were exquisite: golds and reds and greens like the colors in the candy store. I looked to my right, suddenly bombarded with too many images, too much movement in front of me. The colors from the candy display streaked in front of my eyes and moved as I turned my head.

I moved toward the rack of blouses. My hand reached out to touch one of them and just kept going. Farther and farther, it stretched toward the silk fabric until it seemed my hand was no longer a part of me. It kept moving away from me as if disconnected from my arm. The colors of the blouse melted together, forming a horrid, ugly concoction. The patterns, beautifully flowing into each other a moment before, now pushed and clawed against each other, forming grotesque shapes I could no longer make out.

My breath caught suddenly as if I'd been pushed hard against my back, but I was still standing. I looked behind me expecting to see someone, but instead experienced a cacophony of sights and smells and sounds... particularly sounds. I felt as if I was laboring hard to understand, to comprehend something vague and disturbing. I sensed myself being half-in, half-out. Half "here," and half not. The sensations startled me. An impression of myself, young and naive and blissfully ignorant, surrounded me. A me "before." I didn't want to disturb that image, and so remained perfectly still.

Two older ladies shook my shoulders and said that I'd been staring into space for twenty minutes. I felt as if I'd awakened from a dream. I fumbled for words in answer to their puzzled looks, but gave up and ran out of the store into the mall. I was trembling so much I dropped the packages I'd been clutching in my hands. I turned to pick them up. My heart beat wildly. I glanced around, sure that someone, something, was near me, but saw no one.

Reaching my car took forever. I was in a familiar nightmare where, with great effort, I would place one foot in front of me, then the other, then the other ... but with each step, the aisle only became longer, my car farther away. I was loaded with packages and felt as if my feet were made of concrete.

Finally I reached my car. Inside I was safe. Outside I wasn't. So I stayed, with the doors locked, trying to figure out what was happening to me. My heart was racing still, and I could feel the blood pounding through my veins. I tried to calm myself by taking deep breaths, but that was futile. I looked in the rearview mirror. I was sweating, and my eyes were dilated. *How am I going to get home?* I thought. *I need to speak with Phil.*

Phil. My guardian. I felt better just thinking about him. I was so fortunate to have him in my life; it was hard to believe we'd been together for so long. It was hard to believe that I felt my life before I met him, at nineteen, was over. Tall and handsome, his confidence was the first thing that attracted me to him. He was sure of himself, sure of what he wanted, his direction in life. That attracted me, along with his incredible smile and a soft, sensuous curve in his lip.

Well, maybe those two things, his confidence and his smile ... and his deep brown eyes. I could lose myself in his eyes. He was everything in the world that I wanted in a man. Everything. And when he put his arms around me, I felt safe and secure. I needed him to look at me with his brown eyes and tell me I was okay, that I wasn't losing my mind.

I stayed motionless in the car for quite a while, just breathing. Because of the shaking, I wasn't sure I could drive safely. Finally I slammed my hand against the console and pushed the tape button, unsure of what song I'd get. Phoebe Snow. Her soft, sweet voice filled my car and calmed my breathing. With melodic compassion, her words wrapped themselves around my heart and made me feel as if someone understood. The sun moved behind the clouds and a soft rain started falling. I had to get home. I had to talk to Phil.

I'd had a really difficult week, and this ... sensation, or whatever it was ... made me feel worse. I called Phil as soon as I got home, but reached his voice mail. Trying not to sound as if anything was wrong, I asked only that he call me, and told him that I thought perhaps we could get together for lunch. I made a cup of coffee and put his fisherman's sweater on over my own. I felt small and weak and childlike, and needed his arms around me. His sweater was the next best thing; at least it had his smell.

I curled up on a large overstuffed chair near the patio window, drawing my knees up and covering them with Phil's sweater to try to stem my shaking. I kept the lights off in the family room, even though the clouds were quickly moving in front of the sun again, making the sky darker. The family room had become a refuge in the last couple of weeks. It was down two steps from the kitchen and hallway and, because it was sunken, one felt as if they were descending into a nurturing, safe place. It looked out over a lovely garden where we'd planted rosebushes between Victorian-style benches. I told Phil when we planted them in huge planters last summer that the rosebuds reminded me of tiny red kisses with plump, red lips, all strung in a row along the branches.

I watched as the sun moved behind the clouds. The leaves on the patio swirled and danced and lifted themselves toward the treetops as a soft, misty rain stained the patio. This kind of weather always made me feel reflective and moody, but while I usually resisted the feeling, instead I let the haziness seep into me.

The words of the song on the tape came back to me. " ... *I'd hate to be a grown-up and have to try and bear my life in pain.*" A shiver ran down my spine as

I remembered the first time I'd heard that song.

It was New Year's Eve, 1975, in San Francisco. I had met Rob several months earlier, and we had returned to his apartment after a New Year's Eve party.

For so long, I'd had nightmares about Rob, but I hadn't thought of him in years. And when I did, it was only to realize how fortunate I was to not have him in my life any longer.

Rob was like a savory piece of poison candy: good looking and sweet on the outside, but don't bite into it. Don't taste it, because it'll be fatal. And he *was* nice looking and sweet when we first met. He had curly, tousled blond hair and gray eyes with black specks and a really lovely, soft smile. His personality drew me in, along with his smile. He was tall and average in weight, but told me that he'd been overweight as a teenager.

When he told me about the pain and teasing he'd endured, I empathized with him. I'd had the same problem my whole life. When I met him, I was only thirty pounds away from my goal of losing a hundred pounds. I was impressed that he'd accomplished what was so difficult for me, and that he'd kept his weight off for so long. He was a restaurant and beverage manager for a hotel, which made his weight loss even more impressive.

When he asked me back to his apartment after the New Year's Eve party, I didn't have to think twice. Although we'd only known each other a few months, I felt safe with him. I trusted him, and I thought he liked me.

His apartment was a large penthouse overlooking Cathedral Hill and downtown San Francisco. There were no walls; just glass, and at night the lights shone like diamonds. The rain that fell against the windows made them sparkle more brightly. I remember feeling very adult that such a man found me attractive. He'd put his coat over my shoulders when we came up the stairs earlier, and protectively kept rearranging it around me during the evening. Even though I was no longer chilly, I didn't want to take it off. I didn't want him to stop being so attentive and sweet to me.

The living room was sparse so that nothing would compete with the view. A long, elegant couch wound its way the length of one entire wall and along half of the other. An entertainment center along the wall, a marble coffee table, and thick carpeting were about the only other items he had in the living room.

We ended up sitting on the floor talking well into the next morning, he with a glass of champagne, and I with a soft drink. His gentle persuasion to join him in a New Year's drink met with resistance from me, but he was a gentleman and didn't pressure me. I hadn't yet turned eighteen.

Several weeks later, Rob asked if we could see each other more often and, while I enjoyed his company, I was concerned about becoming consumed with our relationship. My mom and I had moved to San Francisco only six months before, and I was captivated with my new life. I was finishing my last year of high school and needed to work full time just to pay bills. But in between, I wanted to experience my new home. The sights, the sounds, the smells of San Francisco... I was in love with it all. And while I really enjoyed going out with Rob, there were things that I wanted to discover on my own. I loved the museums and the library, things that he didn't care for. And sometimes I just wanted to be alone, something he didn't understand.

I needed time to figure out what *I* wanted from life. The concept of not being responsible to anyone but myself was new to me. I felt liberated and unencumbered for the first time in... well, probably forever. Since my parents' divorce during my freshman year, I'd stopped caring. I lost interest in most everything, even school. But now I didn't have the responsibility of trying to keep our tiny family together, and that was a heady feeling; I hadn't realized how much effort it took.

Since moving to San Francisco, though, I was finishing in the top of my senior class, and with some hard work, UC Berkeley would be possible. I was finally beginning to like the person I was becoming. I was starting to discover what *I* wanted.

It was only ten months later that our relationship started to take a terrible turn for the worse. I remembered one particularly bad episode on a city bus...

"Get off. Get off the bus, now!"

I snapped my head around to look at the bus driver. His eyes met mine in the mirror. He was talking to me.

"Yeah, you... get off the bus... don't bring it in here."

Other riders on the bus started yelling at me to get off. I looked through the glass door at Rob. I didn't recognize him any longer. His anger was scaring me. His pupils were dilated, and his face grew more unrecognizable with every moment that passed. His fist slammed against the glass door, then he slammed against several windows, scaring other passengers. Then he returned to the back door when he saw where I was sitting.

I knew that I was in serious trouble. We'd had a fight ... or rather he yelled and I listened. I refused to get into shouting matches; I'd had enough of that with my parents. But this fight was different. Instead of letting it go, instead of letting *me* go, he followed me to the bus stop and, before I could get on the bus, spun me around and slapped my face.

I was astounded. No one had ever hit me before, particularly not someone I knew, someone I trusted, someone I trusted never to hurt me. For all the yelling in my parents' home, their fights never turned physically violent.

My face still stung as I turned around to face the bus driver. "He's ... not my ... I ... can't ..." I was stammering, trying to buy time so the bus driver would give up and drive away, or so someone would come to my rescue. But no one did. Instead, the driver turned to look at me.

"Lady ... now!" He was going to make me get off the bus; he was throwing me back into this with Rob.

I felt as if I was moving in slow motion, but I moved toward the door. I didn't want to get off the bus; I was afraid Rob would hurt me. But I couldn't stay on the bus; clearly, everyone wanted me off because of the scene he was creating. My hand reached for the steel post alongside the door, and I started to walk down the steps. The hiss scared me as the driver released the door, and I looked around at the faces on the bus. I'll never forget their stares, judging me. My eyes implored them to help me, but they wanted to get as far away from Rob as possible.

That day still haunts me. As soon as the bus left, Rob grabbed me by the arm and led me up California Street to a bench overlooking the city. What he told me that day filled me with a terror unlike anything I'd ever known.

"I know where you are every moment of every day," he said. "And if I'm not around, believe me, there are people who are watching you."

I looked at him as if seeing him for the first time. He seemed a completely different man than the one I knew. He noticed me looking at my watch. I was late for my job as manager at a fast food place. I'd never been late before, and had taken pride in the fact that my boss could count on me.

I opened my mouth to speak, but he kept up his tirade. At first I was angry that he'd caused this scene, but he was becoming condemning and judgmental, something I hadn't experienced from him. His sarcasm hurt, reminding me of fights that my parents had had and that I promised I'd never accept in a relationship. I choked back my tears, as much for the sadness of losing a friend and relationship as for the hurt he was causing. I listened, afraid to move, as he went on.

"Your weight, Teresa . . . you're getting too thin." He paced back and forth, back and forth. " . . . and I see how guys look at you . . . Nick . . . Sean . . . I see what they want, and it looks like you want it too."

With each sentence, I grew more distressed. Where was he getting these ideas? As he talked, it became evident he thought I was fooling around . . . or if I hadn't yet, that I was going to. He wasn't seeing *me*, the real me: the insecure, overweight person that I still saw in the mirror. I had noticed guys noticing me more since losing weight, but to me it felt as if they weren't seeing me either. No one wanted me when I was fat, so how could they want me now?

If it hadn't been so terrifying, the change in Rob's personality would have been laughable. *When do I have time to fool around?* I thought to myself. Before I got to school at 7:00 in the morning? During the hour I went home to change at noon and walked to my job? Or maybe on the weekends when I was trying to do extra projects for school so I could get into Berkeley? Since we'd been together, I had struggled hard to focus on what I needed to accomplish. To keep my head above water with bills and save for tuition.

"Why?" he asked. "Why won't you have sex with me? We've been seeing each other for months."

I looked into his eyes. That's what this was all about? I want to make love, not just have sex . . . and that was all this would be. Sex with a companion, not a lover. Everything I'd felt for him dissipated when he slapped me. Everything. How could he expect me to feel anything for him after hurting me?

I didn't want to tell him how much I wanted to make love, how I felt that my sexuality was going to be my undoing, how out of control I felt sometimes. How, as I sat hunched over books, studying in my kitchen, I would watch as a woman across the hall walked naked through her apartment, and the way it made me feel. I wanted to tell him, I wanted to tell *someone*, about how one of my teachers made me feel when he put his arm on my elbow and told me he'd cried when he read my short story. How sexual that made me feel, and how scared at the same time. I needed someone next to me, to hold me. I needed to experience my sexuality. Just not with Rob . . .

The phone jolted me from my memories. It wasn't Phil, but I was back in my home, safe and secure. My time with Rob seemed a lifetime away. The girl I was back then, no longer existed.

I couldn't handle my problems on my own any longer ... as if I ever had. I'd just shoved them down and down and down. And such frightening insomnia, lying awake all night with my mind turning over, rambling thoughts, not making sense.

Several days earlier, I had awakened in a sweat. I couldn't move. Pressed into the mattress, I was unable to even open my mouth to ask Phil for help. I was paralyzed with terror and lay there, dying a terribly violent death. And the smothering sadness.

I needed help. I wanted to wait until after Christmas to make an appointment with the doctor, but everything was unraveling. I had to talk to someone right away, but I was looking in the wrong place; I had to see a psychologist ...

A nurse's voice came over the phone. I don't remember finding the number for my HMO in the phone book or making the call. I just can't remember. The cool wood of the cabinets felt good against my back as I slid to the kitchen floor, stretching the phone cord even further.

I couldn't catch my breath, and I heard my heart pounding in my ears as I talked to her. Even now, I can recall her name and the inflection in her voice. Calming and gentle, she asked how she could help.

The words spilled out of me, hesitantly at first, then, when I encountered no resistance, they came in a torrent. I hadn't noticed how cold the floor was against my thighs until I took another breath.

"The only thing is, I'd like to see a man." I said it without thinking, and wasn't even sure why I'd said it. The appointment she offered was more than a month away, but her insistence that I wait for Gary, more a statement than an option, instilled trust. He was, she said, the best and worth waiting for.

As soon as I hung up, I was apprehensive. I'd made a decision. A decision solely for me, something I hadn't done in some time. I felt broken and disembodied and disappointed in myself that I needed help. I was scared at opening myself up to a stranger. I wouldn't be able to accept his rejection, but the effect of what had happened cast an eerie shadow over my marriage, over my life, in the rage that I carried inside me. I had thought I was free; I was not.

So I'd taken the first step of placing my fragile self in someone else's hands, and I felt a sense of surrender. After hanging up the phone, I felt an immediate sense of non-responsibility. It was strange ... like deciding to start a diet on

Monday and thinking you had all weekend to eat all you wanted because the decision was out of your hands, so you could let yourself go. I could think anything I wanted to now; I could slide over the edge because I knew there was someone out there who would help me.

I put Gary's name and phone number on the calendar and circled it in red ink, counting the days until I would see him. It was 2:00 already, and Phil still hadn't called. Then I remembered that he'd mentioned a meeting that morning before leaving.

I made another cup of coffee, took the cordless phone, and went upstairs to the guest bedroom. If the family room had become a womb-like refuge in the past several weeks, the guest bedroom was slowly becoming even more so. While a winter cold could snake through the first floor, this guest bedroom on the upper floor remained toasty warm. Golden sunlight often streamed through the window, nourishing the deep green ivy, grown huge with tender loving care, that we'd placed on the night tables.

We'd decorated this bedroom with colors that were in sharp contrast to the rest of the house. Deep hunter green and vivid burgundy melded together, inviting our guests to relax and enjoy their stay, while the rest of the house was more light and airy. Phil and I joked that we must have gotten hungry when decorated, buying curtains and furniture with colors like French Vanilla and Sweet White Chocolate. The rest of the room was decorated in the same colors. An elaborate patchwork of designs echoed off the thick goosedown comforter, and again off the curtains.

And then again, I realized for the first time, off the fabric covering the boxes against the wall.

Sitting cross-legged on the bed, I stared at the group of boxes in front of me. The rain tapped ever so softly against the window, and the room grew darker still to match my mood. The sun moved deeper behind the clouds.

Anniversaries. They became more and more important to me as a means of measurement. How far I'd come. How far I still had to go. I kept count as one who was imprisoned. Mentally ticking away the weeks. The months. The years. I looked at my past, not to savor but to judge.

My means to that end was a secret journey into boxes we'd carried along with us everywhere we moved over the past seventeen years. The boxes sat innocently in pretty, flowered fabric. I'd stacked them in a pyramid and topped them with a menagerie of my stuffed animals.

The animals sat in front of me now, guarding the boxes. A family brought together by mostly difficult times in my life, they fulfilled a unique promise from the gift giver: warmth, comfort, love, nurturing, to soothe a broken heart. The fuzzy, sweet bunny with a pink bow and collar, my first from Phil. The smallest, a cream-colored teddy bear with soft brown eyes I'd bought when I was pregnant. And a playful panda that Phil brought in perched atop his shoulders to cheer me up after surgery.

The stuffed animals guarded my memories for me, memories contained in boxes that had become a metaphor for how I'd dealt with the pain. Wrap the pain in pretty fabric. Let it stack up. Put it away where I'm sure not to see it.

I'd tried to compartmentalize my memories, to arrange the sequence of events in order to comprehend, but there was no logic, no orderliness to what had happened to me. Placing like items together in boxes didn't help; categorizing the items didn't help, nor did labeling them. I'd become exhausted by my attachment to the boxes, by what was inside.

I needed to open them one last time in order to share my life, my past, my self, with my husband.

Despair over my inability to handle my emotions had finally led me to search for a psychologist and take this final step: to open the boxes and look inside. Questions frustrated me, for which I found no answer, no blueprint, no road map. How was I to accept what had happened?

When my husband's hands, lips, body were on top of mine, I needed to feel *him*, experience *him*. I found my way during our relationship, albeit clumsily, and made a lot of mistakes along the way. My identity, though negative, was at least familiar. It dictated my behavior, because it was my view of how I believed others would see me and judge me. *They* identified me. Or so I'd come to believe.

But the time had come for me to trust another person and learn a different, more effective way to deal with the pain of what had happened. The package in which I had neatly tucked my rage and shame and covered carefully with beautiful fabric, was unraveling.

Chapter 2

December, 1994

Phil and I sat on the couch in the living room.

I loved this room. Because it was sunken, two steps down from the dining room, the ceiling seemed to stretch toward the sky. And the fireplace, deep green marble, was in deep contrast to the soft beige hue of almost everything else in the room.

But the house had become my prison. We'd moved in only three years earlier, and while I didn't think it was the last house we'd own, I thought we'd be there quite a while. It was a Victorian and painted a beautiful, soft pastel pink with slightly darker trim. Pretty roses nestled against an old-fashioned porch in the front. Very much the dream house, and very much worth the time and effort necessary to make the dream ours, it was one of four built in colors of candy: soft pink, green, yellow, and orange. Our tiny development looked like a child's play set of Victorian dollhouses.

A huge, two-story foyer with warm, taffy-colored hardwood floors was framed on one side by the kitchen, and then two steps down, a family room. On the other side was a dining room, and then two steps down again, the living room. On all the paned windows and on the beveled stained glass front door hung delicate lace curtains, allowing the softest glow of the fading sunset to rest on the inside of the house.

"Shall I start a fire?" Phil got up and moved to the fireplace.

"No, I'm okay ... I just want to talk," I said, reaching for his hand as he sat next to me. I was hesitant to continue without some sort of ... prelude, I suppose. But I went on without much thought of how to frame my proposal.

"I need help. Help from a professional and ... I've made an appointment. I think he's the best. Is that okay?"

I needed Phil to agree to the therapy before I began; in fact, I needed him to think it was a really good idea. I'd put him in an uncomfortable position, though. There was a part of me that wanted him to say no. That would've allowed me to hide from my feelings for a while longer. But the more rational part of me knew that he would agree to whatever I felt was best. He knew I didn't rush into situations without thinking first, and he respected my intelligence in being able to think through a problem. And this *was* best for me.

"You know ... I think it's a great idea. You've been so ... sad lately ... " Phil was extremely intuitive, and I couldn't believe I'd actually thought he hadn't seen what was going on. "What you might like to do," he went on, taking my hands in his, "you might like to write down how you're feeling and take that to your first appointment. You'll probably be a little nervous. If you don't get everything out the first day, don't worry about it. Take the time you need to feel better. Maybe you'd like to go out tonight for dinner. We can stop at Barnes & Noble afterwards."

Logic mixed with tenderness. Practicality with a large dash of compassion. That describes my husband. I lived in a chaotic house as a child, and I was more than a little surprised, and delighted, by Phil's solid, calm nature. What a rare union of left-brain, right-brain abilities. As a software designer for more than twenty-five years, he'd sharpened those skills so much so that nothing seemed to surprise him. And those traits surfaced at just the right moment, along with his keen sense of humor, to make anyone feel at ease.

From the first, I admired my husband's personality, his traits. It seemed that his strengths were my weaknesses. Whereas I knew guilt and shame intimately, he didn't subscribe to those concepts at all. Whereas I tended to be hypercritical of myself, particularly in terms of my body, my accomplishments, my performance, he presented the exact opposite. On occasions when he was at fault, he accepted responsibility, rectified the situation quickly, and moved on with no loss of self-esteem. Whereas Phil was extremely extroverted and outgoing, and rarely edited his past, I was more introverted and moody, desperately trying to rewrite mine.

Since calling for the appointment with Gary, my "symptoms" — for lack of a better word — were frightening. My concentration dissipated like steam escaping through my ears while working. I just couldn't focus. I'd been in a highly technical field for years. We owned our own software design firm, and I really enjoyed my work. But I felt as if I was a baby, regressing in knowledge rather than advancing.

I'd lost interest in almost everything but Phil, and would've been content sitting in an empty, dark theater with him and a huge tub of popcorn, just watching movies all day. I felt ashamed of my lack of motivation, and scared when I couldn't modify my behavior with willpower. I had gone through other bad periods in my life, of course, but never like this. When anxious, I longed for numbness, and vice versa. My feelings swung wildly from polar opposites.

Something else was wrong, too. I was having strange thoughts about something catastrophic happening, particularly in the house. I succumbed to a sickening ritual that was driving me nuts. Before leaving the house, I had to check to make sure something, such as a curling iron or hair dryer, was unplugged. Not certain that I'd *really* turned it off, I'd go downstairs, then return upstairs, then down, then up, then down, then up. Ten times, fifteen times, twenty times. No matter how many times I'd return to check out the appliance, I didn't believe what I saw.

So I tried to work around the problem by leaving the house when Phil left. Then, further into the behavior, I'd *tell* him, then *show* him physically that I'd unplugged the appliance. Then it got really bad. I started asking him to check the appliances *for* me. It was humiliating, but I couldn't control my fear, and Phil was mystified. He couldn't figure out why I'd become so irrational. I panicked at the thought of leaving the house because something might happen, and I was becoming really alarmed about my sanity.

Most of all, I was frightened by what felt like an uncontrollable urge to eat. The impulse to force something down with food was intense, and I felt out of control. As soon as I finished one meal, I began thinking about the next. I couldn't regulate myself and didn't know whether I was hungry or satiated. I didn't know whether I could stop or not — and if I could stop, whether I'd be able to survive, to exist. It was a painful feeling that consumed my day.

Each day I'd pick up the phone to cancel the appointment with Gary, and each day I'd put it back down again. I became incapable of making decisions, even tiny ones. I vacillated between being happy that I'd made the appointment, and miserable that I'd made the appointment, terrified at bringing up things that might be better left alone. I felt the need to hold onto what I knew, as negating and oppressive as it was, because it was a known.

But the feeling that was most alarming, the one that scared me most and kept me from canceling the appointment, was the feeling that I wanted to hurt myself. I was frantic to begin therapy.

Before I'd begun, I started worrying about what the ending looked like. How would I know when I was *"cured"* ... when my problem had been *"fixed?"* Something was seriously wrong, but the problems I'd had were long ago and far away. It was so long ago ... I was over it. I really was. *People have been through worse, and besides, my life is really going well.* Those thoughts went through my mind nearly every day. The last several years had been difficult for many reasons, but the depression was inescapable. I needed to make a change in my life.

I thought about each possible scenario for my first appointment with Gary. One possibility was that he would hear me out, sit back in his huge leather chair and declare me pitifully weak and self-centered, and proceed to tell me how I was taking time from others who really needed his services. Another possibility: alarm would register on his face and he would declare me over the edge, a danger to myself. Before I knew what was happening, I'd be placed in a padded room. My logical mind brewed under the surface, but I would have none of it.

Memories were etched into my mind, but I questioned how I might take this psychologist into a journey inside myself. How was I to provide him with the colors, the sounds, the smells? How was I to relate the feelings that were tearing at my flesh? I was anxious for the sake of my marriage to do whatever was necessary, but I hadn't a clue as to how to go about it.

Several days later, after Phil left for work, I couldn't get started. I was exhausted and lay down on the couch in the living room. I barely recognized this room in the daylight. Now, since becoming frightened, I restricted where I went in the house when I was alone, so I spent most of the time in the kitchen and family room.

I looked around. The sun danced through the long lace curtains that Phil and I hung the past summer. I was so exhausted. All I wanted to do was sleep. I lay down on the couch and let the sun wash over me. No music. No TV. Just silence. And the sound of my breath and my heartbeat.

The dream, an incredibly detailed, lovely image, came to me often in my life. When I closed my eyes, I saw no grotesque figures, no nightmares, just my dream ...

My husband and I are living along the ocean. The scene is always the same in my mind. The room, a library next to a kitchen in which my husband and I sit, is bathed in a soft glow from the fireplace. The walls are covered from floor to ceiling with books, making the room seem dark and warm. There are shutters on the windows. They're open slightly, but it's gotten dark early because it's wintertime.

I'm lying stretched out on a huge, buttery-soft, hunter green leather chair with my feet up on an ottoman. Both have the look and smell and feel of soothing comfort, the look and smell and feel of one of my dad's old bomber jackets. A couch is at a right angle to the chair and a soft, ecru, fleece blanket is tossed over it. In front of me is a large, square coffee table made of mahogany that holds books of our favorite artists and some candles which I've lit. My face is flushed as the flames from the candle and fireplace dance toward me.

Phil is sitting behind me in a leather chair that matches the other furniture, behind a huge mahogany desk. I hear his fingers methodically clicking the keyboard, and I hear him humming softly to some music in the background. He's trust and security and warmth and love. He's my soul, and I know that, should we live that long, we'll be friends and lovers into our eighties, nineties. I look forward to knowing him, to learning even more about him than I know now.

Beside me is a beautiful Irish setter, so close to me I can feel her breath on my leg. I run my hands along her fur; it's silken and warm. She's loyalty and absolute friendship, judging me not by how I look or what I accomplish. She loves my touch and stays near me.

The smell of something good fills the air, and we're waiting for friends who are visiting for the weekend. And as always in this dream, my hand falls to my stomach, full and large. I'm pregnant with our ...

I bolted upright, awakened by a noise. My heart was pounding. I sensed someone outside on the porch, and realized the noise must have been the doorbell. It rang again and again, more insistent each time. I didn't move. It kept ringing until I nearly gave up and answered it, certain that the person knew I was inside, afraid and hiding. But I was nailed to the couch; I couldn't move.

Then it stopped. I saw a silhouette of the person through the lace curtains. He turned and walked down the steps of the porch. My breathing didn't return to normal, nor did I move.

Phil's car in the driveway woke me from my thoughts. Phil. His role in my life, and mine in his, was still a mystery to me.

Chapter 3

January 1995

I set out for the 9:00 appointment at 7:30 ... to go ten miles. I didn't want to be late. I needn't have worried; I arrived at Gary's office at 8:00 and drove around the neighborhood ... then parked in the parking lot ... then drove around some more until his building opened. It was a mistake being there. The time I'd spent calmly recalling facts, rehearsing my story over and over in my own mind during the past five weeks, had been a waste of time. My mind was a blank.

The waiting room was bathed in soothing colors and lights and bountiful green plants. The receptionist, well trained at calming fragile nerves, was warm and did her best to make me feel at ease.

I picked up a *Time* magazine but couldn't concentrate enough to read an entire article, so I sat just flipping the pages and speculating about the other patients in the waiting room. What brought them here? The couple in the corner... marital problems? Or perhaps a dying parent or a sick child? The young man on the other side of the room looked so sad. A girlfriend who'd left him, or a problem at work? Compassion washed over me for whatever had brought them here. I glanced again at the young couple and noticed their clothing, then looked at my own. I hadn't realized that I'd dressed up more formally than usual. Had I wanted to make a good impression?

"Teresa?"

I jumped. I'd become hypersensitive to people surprising me, a loud voice or noise, and it bothered me tremendously. I thought I'd had it pretty much under control, but like so many other things . . . no, I didn't.

Gary was tall and attractive and had a confident manner about him. He was impeccably dressed. His eyes met mine directly, and he had a sort of shy but completely engaging smile. I'd been told by the nurse that he was the head of the department, but I was surprised to see that he was only about ten years older than I. There was a part of me, I suppose, that wanted him to be old and not very good looking, but he was quite the opposite.

His office was spacious and comforting, with a beautiful view of the mountains through a window behind the couch. Abundant bundles of brilliant flowers snuggled against the outside of the building beneath his window. He offered me a seat and a glass of water and, while he went down the hall to get it, I took a moment to look around the room. An immense bookshelf and several photographs gave me the sense that he was well-read and enjoyed traveling.

Gary returned with my glass of water, and sat down in front of me. He leaned back, casually crossing his legs. I was glad to see that one of us was at ease. I noticed that his shoes were very fashionable and highly polished. *He's meticulous*, I thought. That's something I appreciate in people.

My eyes darted around the room, unable to meet his, something uncharacteristic for me. My anxiety was at such a peak that I had expected my words to come tumbling from my mouth as soon as we'd met, that I would be unable to stop talking. Or crying. That was my other fear, that I would begin crying in front of him and be unable to stop.

I carefully responded to his answers, providing basic descriptors. *Married to a fantastic man for eleven years, but together for eighteen. His name is Phil. Software designer. Self-employed. No children.* I heard myself talk as if I was a different person. Looking into his eyes was difficult, until I realized that he probably couldn't see very well into mine with the light behind me.

Although he was considerate and friendly and kept the conversation moving forward through my nervous laughs and too-sparse account of my history, I was nonetheless intimidated by him. I feared that he would find me weak or stupid. Or worse, crazy. But I was desperate for his help. I heard the words I'd carefully rehearsed, yet they seemed disconnected and strangely lacking emotion. I felt nauseous suddenly, and wanted to tell him that I was okay, that this was all a big mistake, that I was sorry for taking his time. I dreaded saying it even more, though, because it wouldn't have been true and I'd never be able to get the help I needed.

We evaluated each other ... or rather, our ability to work together. A dance, of sorts. He was determining, I suppose, how he could best help me and I was gaining trust in him so that I could tell him my secrets. I knew this about myself: that I was determined, and if I began therapy with Gary, it would be because I felt he was the best. This was going to be an unfamiliar experience for me, and I had to trust that he was the right one to guide me through it.

A secret: *Something kept from the knowledge of others,* according to Websters. I wanted to share more of myself with Gary that day. I'd kept everything inside for so long. It became inconceivable to keep these secrets from Phil, but I'd lived so long in the fear that he'd leave me if he knew what had really happened. But I needed to share it with him. My first step, though, my rehearsal, would have to be with Gary.

I called Phil as soon as I got home and asked if he could meet me for lunch. I didn't have to return to my client that day, since I'd worked late into the evening the previous night, trying to take my mind off everything.

"I've arranged for us to go down to Monterey for the weekend," he said as soon as I got into the car. I relaxed into the seat, ecstatic that he said he had time, and could even take the rest of the day off with me if I liked. "You know," he went on, turning to face me, "I want you to know that you can talk about it if you want, or you don't have to. Whatever you're comfortable with. I just want you to know that I'm here for you, whatever you decide."

I looked over at him and nodded. "Yeah ... I would like to talk later, I think. Gary was really nice and ... he was friendly to me. I'm not going to see him for three more weeks." I lowered my eyes and tried not to cry. "Thank you so much for taking us to Monterey this weekend. I really appreciate it." I leaned over to kiss him.

I'd so looked forward to this appointment, and now it was over. I was disappointed that I wouldn't be able to see Gary again for so long. *Too* long. I'd waited hundreds of hours for this one small hour. It was over nearly before it began. I was exhausted.

Chapter 4

March, 1995

My acceptance to graduate school was untimely, with my decision to begin therapy. But getting my master's degree and then my doctorate had been a lifelong dream. My plans had been delayed *for* me last time, but now, nothing short of an act of God was going to stop me. And it was a diversion from therapy.

Still, my feelings were overwhelming. I vacillated with every small detail. *Should I tell Gary about ...? And then that will lead to ... But I'm not sure that's really important. Or is it? Does it hold the key to what's happening to me?*

Confusion. Information was constantly filtered through my eyes, of course ... *my* version of history, *my* recollection of emotions and their significance.

I'd had two more appointments. I was on my fourth now, and still resisted talking about my past. I thought constantly about the huge task Gary had in front of him trying to figure *me* out, and I analyzed the question of whether I should bring up my history. *Not important*, I decided. *Too long ago. Can't do anything about it now, anyway.*

Gary continued to try to put me at ease, and while I wanted to open up to him, I struggled against it. I knew I was free to say whatever was on my mind, but found that I became pithy and insightful when by myself and quiet when with him. *This is backwards*, I would think, sitting in his office. *Talk ... talk ... talk out loud, dammit. He's never going to be able to help you if you don't open your mouth.*

The thought that he was judging me was always with me, probably reinforcing my resistance. I had the nagging thought that he would think I was wasting his time when I couldn't articulate what I felt or what I needed from him. I had no practice in asking for what I needed, so my needs went unmet. It wasn't his fault, but mine. I liked him and respected him, though, and was curious what he thought of me.

"How am I going to know I'm done . . . how do we measure our success with this?" I asked one day.

He gave me a quizzical smile, as if I was a dinner guest getting up to leave after the soup. I understood the look. We hadn't even finished our appetizers, and I was ready for my coat.

"Why is it important to measure . . . to know when you're done?"

"Ah . . ." A sigh escaped from me. I knew better than to ask a direct question without having done the work to get the answer on my own. But this had been on my mind. How *would* I know when I was finished? I knew I wasn't yet, but how does one know? I'd lived in a world of facts, figures, measurables, quotas, of criteria and proof. Of standards and tests. This all seemed *very* gray to me. To the extent that I could understand him, I needed an explanation.

I needed to bridge his world to mine, and so relied on the solidity of familiarity. To step outside myself and hear myself speak, I was certain it seemed as if my head was on straight; yet it was the farthest thing from the truth. I was deceiving myself, or trying to, and he would have none of it.

Conflict was evident in my every action. I *felt* like screaming, yet could only smile politely and nod. I *felt* like reaching out to him, yet kept my distance. I *felt* like getting serious, yet made nervous jokes, hiding (in *my* mind, anyway) my discomfort, constantly wondering what he thought of me. I was conscious of a peculiar feeling of being trapped and wanting to escape. When my freedom was in danger of compromise, I chose retreat.

I returned home from my appointment intending to work on a project I'd been putting off. I was too restless. *This isn't working,* I thought. *I'm not cooperating or . . . something.* I went upstairs and changed into jeans and a blouse and wandered through the house, trying to figure out why I was so restless and irritated. *I'm just not cooperating,* I thought again. And I *wasn't.* I felt like a fraud when I was in his office. There was so much I wanted to say to him, and I needed his help. I waited for him to ask the question that would draw everything out of me, yet he couldn't know what the question was. I was in a loop, and becoming discouraged. I had to make the next move.

I grabbed a soda and went back upstairs to the guest room. It was unseasonably warm, and I opened a window to let a soft breeze blow in through lace curtains and the sun dance off the comforter. Suddenly I became aware of my need to look through the boxes. I *had* to, in order to move to the next step with Gary. I didn't have a choice.

I lay back on the bed, taking a moment to assess the job ahead of me. At times, like today with Gary, I felt an almost overwhelming lack of emotion, and at other times, my sensitivity was razor sharp. I wasn't sure which was worse, but I was terrified that once I let the feelings come, they weren't going to stop. The cards, letters, legal papers in the boxes, and especially the white envelope, all held my secrets from seventeen years ago. They all explained the person I'd become.

The night before was incredibly long. Old ghosts invaded me as I slept. The nightmare had started as a dream . . .

My dad had just died. I was inconsolable. I was in a house with my mom, who had just gotten some men to agree to further research. Suddenly I was in a VA hospital with my husband, giving blood for a test. I looked down at my left leg and saw a cut. I looked over at my right leg and saw a huge scab. All in one piece. I carefully pulled it from my leg, keeping it in one long piece, and wrapped it onto itself. I asked some psychologists who were nearby what I should do with it. What was it? I ran from doctor to doctor, looking for answers. The urge to run was becoming intense, as was the feeling of being trapped.

The pain of continuing as I had became agonizing, and I knew that discomfort in the process of healing was unavoidable. Rationalization had become a means of delaying the inevitable, the way I avoided telling my secrets.

I returned to my task of opening the first box. I approached my job as logically as possible and planned my strategy. *Take off the cover. Look inside. Address the contents. Deal with the feelings. Simple. Clean. Over.* My brightly colored, beautifully decorated boxes were full of memories too horrible to look at, let alone comprehend. *Crime, Betrayal, Death, Birth* . . . they were all terribly dramatic, but all too frighteningly true. I'd kept the boxes meticulously wrapped, taking care to cover every inch in a glorious union of deep hunter green and vibrant burgundy. My stuffed animals stared back at me, guardians of my memories.

A piece of paper inside the first box was labeled *Before*. Perhaps it was my natural inclination toward organization, but just as likely it was meant to be a warning sign for my own eyes on my next journey inside, as if to say, "Don't bother entering... you won't like what you find." And under the sheet of paper declaring the contents of the first box was a large white envelope warning anyone who dared to venture inside ... *DON'T OPEN ... EVER.* I put it aside. I remember writing those words. I remember writing what's inside. I remember far too much, yet not enough.

I took a deep breath ...

The train schedule when my mom and I moved from Michigan to California in August 1974. The itinerary of a trip to a retreat I took with my class during my senior year of high school, just after moving. A set of shiny keys to my first apartment, and a small, delicate necklace that Rob had given me before everything started changing between us. And ... in my hand, a letter from Rob dated June 17, 1976, the day my life changed forever.

I felt a sensation of being pulled away ... further outside of myself as memories flooded my mind. I was dizzy and couldn't catch my breath. I looked around the room; it was spinning wildly. My hand groped for the cover of the box. I slammed the cover hard down onto the box, afraid the memories inside would suddenly explode.

I can't do this now, I thought. *I can't do this ... I can't do this.* I fell back on the bed. The memories were safely hidden again, but I was nauseous. I lay on the bed, afraid to move for fear of being sick, until Phil came home.

Chapter 5

June, 1995

Gary was late for our appointment, and I felt horrible. He mentioned that he had a client who needed his time, and I felt small and insignificant and as if I didn't matter at all. Familiar feelings.

It was June already, six months into therapy, and I was feeling more disjointed than ever. Nothing was moving except my weight, and that was just moving up. Memories of ugly times in my life were with me, but in a vague and chaotic way. I felt restless and trapped and upset, and then more upset that I was putting Phil through this as well.

While I usually planned what I was going to talk to Gary about on our next appointment, I hadn't wanted to even *think* about this session.

"I finally had my appointment with Dr. Long." I blurted it out before I'd reached Gary's couch, ignoring the usual pleasantries. I was irritated. He'd referred me to Dr. Long, a gynecologist, several months earlier when he became concerned about some medical problems I was having. I remember feeling optimistic about my appointment. I'd never been referred by another doctor before and was certain that I'd receive more comprehensive—no—special, treatment, since Dr. Long was a colleague.

I was wrong. And I was irritated, and it showed. *Perhaps this is a consequence of therapy*, I remember thinking. *If so, well, he's the professional. Isn't this what he wanted? My true feelings?* Just as quickly, I was ashamed of myself. But

I had trusted Gary with my feelings, and the treatment I received from Dr. Long was extremely hurtful. I slid into a feeling of self-pity. Another person pissing me off. Another person telling me by his actions that my feelings didn't matter. That *I* didn't matter.

I brought my hands up, rubbing my forehead. My head ached, and I gulped to get some air into my lungs. My mouth opened to speak. I was surprised to hear myself talking to Gary about Rob . . .

Rob. He's the one who pissed me off. Big time. Rob was highly practiced at being annoying, irritating, obnoxious, and generally all around toxic to my health. I felt so trapped, so impotent when faced with certain men.

I was seventeen when I met Rob. I spoke with him the afternoon that it happened. 2:30 sharp. As always, he wanted to know where I was going that evening, and with whom. He had become so critical of my every move. I know it wasn't always that way. Like anyone, I suppose, in a relationship like this, I hadn't noticed the quantum leap he'd taken from small, isolated jealous outbursts to the possessive paranoia that he'd been displaying lately.

It was Thursday. He knew where I was. Working, like I was every day. And he knew where I was going that night. To Elaine's for a photography class. I heard myself promise that I would call him as soon as I got home. I remember thinking that was odd because if he was a lover, I would have been thrilled that he couldn't go to sleep without knowing I was safe. But I felt nothing.

I worked at a small photography studio in the Castro district. My boss, Rick, was sweet and kind, and offered to help a friend and me with our photography on Thursdays. Tall and sort of lanky, but heavier than what "lanky" implies, he had an engaging smile and eyes that shone when he laughed. They were always moist. I don't think I'd ever seen him angry or cross at anyone. I loved his stability, his lack of moodiness.

Rob was becoming more and more unpredictable, though, and I wondered how long I'd be able to meet them on Thursdays. Last week he'd called me at Elaine's home and hassled me about something or other. Four times, he called. It was humiliating and embarrassing.

We picked Elaine's apartment for our weekly meetings because of its "photographic potential." Rick's words. She lived near Golden Gate Park in a huge Victorian converted to flats. It was painted purple and yellow, and reminded me of a huge, lovely violet straining toward the sky. It was just as beautiful inside. Heavy mahogany, even in the kitchen, mixed with her funky furniture. It was warm and cozy, and I loved being there.

Elaine was a mother-earth type. She was petite in size, but her heart was huge. She had long, kinky hair to her waist that looked as if she never combed it, but you just wanted to touch that hair. She had a sweet seven-year-old daughter who she was raising on her own. Recently let go from a dance troupe because of a knee injury, she was having real difficulty, so Rick and I took turns bringing dinner. I know she knew what was going on, but we insisted that because she let us use her house, we had to at least pay for dinner.

Our only problem: we had such a good time being together that we rarely photographed the "potential" outside. We had a ritual. After dinner, Rick would critique the photos we'd taken through the week and, in mock exasperation, throw the photos in a pile in the center of the table. We hadn't "gotten" his vision, he would say with a crooked grin. He loved being our Svengali.

I had something on my mind since talking to Rob, though, and told Rick that I'd meet him at Elaine's apartment at 5:30. I always left early on Thursdays to make pick-ups and deliveries, and asked Rick if he could order the pizza for me, that I'd pay him when I got there.

I pushed the delivery packets into my backpack and hopped on a bus. It was already busy going into downtown San Francisco, and I had to stand.

"I'm going to fuck you this weekend, you little whore."

Rob's words burned into my mind. He'd never spoken to me like that. He never called me that before, and it really stung. It hurt as bad as when he'd slapped my face last year. Nothing I said calmed him down, and nothing I did made him leave me alone.

His temper was more erratic than ever. It seemed like things that wouldn't have bothered him when we first met were starting to really get on his nerves. Sometimes it was directed at me, but mostly it was directed outward at his friends or people who worked for him. I didn't like being with him anymore. It was too scary.

Sex with Rob. No. Sex with anyone would've taken me way off my goals. I'd just picked up the admissions packet and catalog from UC Berkeley the previous week, and pored over it again and again. The thin paper of the catalog was no match for me. I was thirsty for all it promised. The classes sounded exciting: Freud and Jung, The Psychology of Personality, and Developmental Psychology. I never thought I'd be exposed to such opportunities. Even though I couldn't attend for another year, a friend and I took the BART train over to the bookstore every Friday night to buy books for the classes. We'd stop at a pizza place and read the class descriptions to each other. I prayed that I would be accepted and be able to move to Berkeley. Being away from Rob would be better for both of us. Well, certainly better for me.

I was excited about getting together with Rick and Elaine that evening. Rick had submitted some of our photos to the owners of some galleries he knew, and he'd told me earlier that day that he had some exciting news for us.

I got downtown in about a half hour and made several deliveries. I made my last stop at a camera store, where I bought a present for Elaine: two lens filters she'd really wanted.

My next stop was my favorite bookstore on Montgomery, around the corner from the camera store. I didn't have a lot of time, but it was so close so . . . I just couldn't resist. Perusing the bookshelves left only a moment at home to feed my kitty, and grab some more money. I was in a hurry, and my purse was already full with my book and my package for Elaine. And then . . .

"This doesn't matter . . . I meant to tell you about San Francisco," I said to Gary. I interrupted my own story. I was surprised that I'd started talking about this. It was so insignificant. I'd really wanted to tell him what Phil and I had done the prior weekend. That was more important, in my mind. Phil and Rob. The contrast was startling; one couldn't get much different than the other.

I'm sure my irritation that I'd wasted time talking about Rob was evident, and I didn't want it to be. I just wanted to be important to Gary at that moment. While some days I had barely seven words to say, that day I was on a roll. Lately, I'd felt as if I'd been assigned a task to do with no tools, no outline, no specs. My work was built on specifications, and when there were none . . . well, I wasn't sure how to proceed.

"Please . . ." he invited me to continue.

Last weekend started well . . . it was an anniversary for me. June 17th. It just happened to fall on Saturday. Phil told me he wanted to replace my bad memories with good ones, and that he was taking me to San Francisco. At first, I sort of panicked. It didn't seem right to be going back to a place with so many memories. But he'd made the arrangements, and I really wanted to go. Perhaps this was the best thing for me.

The hotel lobby of the Fairmont was exquisite. Gold and marble. That's all that one's eyes see. It felt as if we'd been transported back in time. And the room. It looked out onto the bay and out to Sausalito. Coit Tower was on our right, standing like a beacon atop Telegraph Hill. We fell onto the bed when the bellman left, and hugged each other. If anyone could turn this experience, this memory, around, it was Phil.

We decided that since it was early, we'd go downtown and do some shopping and then come back for dinner at the hotel in the Tonga Room. We walked down Powell Street. In a way, it felt as if I was home. I hadn't been in the city for so long.

When we came back, we were tired. It had turned quite chilly, so we decided to take a cab back to the hotel. When we got inside, we fell onto the bed again and watched television for a while. Having Phil so close to me, it's difficult not to feel like making love, so we did. Afterwards, as Phil called room service for dinner, I slipped into a hot bath. The view, having made love, dinner, and champagne made for a wonderfully relaxing evening.

Phil turned to me later in the evening. "I think maybe we should go past the house. What do you think? Do you want to face it? Are you ready?"

My heart did a flip-flop. I hadn't thought so. I hadn't thought I was ready a moment ago ... but now, all relaxed with Phil. I was ready to try.

Later, I tossed and turned, unable to fall asleep, thinking about the house and all the horror that had happened there, so many years ago, and woke Phil again when I brought my hand around him and hugged him tight. I asked if he would make love to me again, and it was with a passion and energy that contradicted how tired I'd become. I felt as if we were one person, and I never wanted it to end. Still, the thoughts were with me: was I helping myself by going by that house? Was this the right move? I had no way of knowing.

The next morning, Phil asked if I'd changed my mind. I told him I hadn't, and he said that in any case, he wanted to treat me to brunch before we left. The view from the top of the Fairmont was breathtaking. Looking out over San Francisco, it was hard to believe that the city held the terrifying memories it did for me. But Phil was right: whatever happened next, the trip had been worth it. He'd succeeded in helping make June 17 mean something different to me.

After brunch and check-out, we got in the car and headed down Sacramento Street, driving past my old apartment. It was just as it had been, as if no time had passed at all. The front of the apartment house was a facade of red brick, with two large windows on either side of the entrance. The two on the left side of the building on the first floor were mine. I loved that apartment, until ... well, seeing it again reminded me of so much.

We drove past Polk Street and up the hill, still on Sacramento. Too soon, we were there. Just off the corner where the house used to sit. Used to sit. I couldn't believe it had been replaced with a newer, more modern apartment building. It had been seventeen years, but still ... I wasn't prepared for this. It was gone!

Something snapped inside me. Where was it? I wanted to see it. I'd worked so hard, I'd come so far to confront this ghost, and now it was gone. I'd had this feeling before, this feeling of facing something and having it turn out to be a shadow.

I turned to Phil. His eyes were warm and compassionate, and he took hold of my hands. I suppose he could see the disappointment on my face, or the ... I'm not really sure what I felt at that moment. I didn't know who I was any more. I didn't know what to feel, or where to go. I just didn't know, and the confusion was really painful.

My time with Gary was up already. Too soon.

I returned home in an angry mood and worked my way upstairs. Guys pissing me off. Gary had warned me that it would get worse before it got better. He had written some sayings on a paper for me to keep in my wallet. His familiar handwriting pierced the paper with strong, hard strokes in some places and lighter, more gentle strokes in others. The paper, which eventually became torn and creased and folded dozens of times over, became something tangible for me, something real to hold onto.

His words consoled me, and I allowed them to come to me as he would, were he there with me: *"I did the best I could." "I had no choice." "I'm not a bad person because things happen to me." "Things may feel worse for a while as we take the 'lids' off of what you have repressed or denied." "Panic comes from the sense or feeling of loss of control." "All these feelings are me."*

I folded the paper and put it back in my wallet. *If only you could understand what I've been through ... what I've done,* I thought. But it would have to wait until our next appointment.

Chapter 6

August, 1995

My symptoms had returned. All of them. Plus. I hung my head in the sink in the bathroom off the family room. I was nauseous and clammy. Hyperventilating. My elbows pressed against the edge of the sink were tender, but I couldn't move. I stayed that way for a long time, just looking into the sink, down the drain, out of our home, into the river, out to the sea . . . I was lost.

I'd been on the way to the store when I jumped out of the car. *Did I turn off the curling iron?* Grabbing my keys, I ran to the bathroom. Yes, it was turned off. I turned and walked out the garage door. I sat down in the car and put the key in the ignition. *Is it really turned off?* I got out of the car again, unlocked the door to the house and ran to the bathroom. Yes. It was turned off. I turned again to go to the door. This time I didn't get to the car before turning around. *Is it unplugged? What if it's not? It could start a fire.* Back I turned toward the bathroom before I knew what had grabbed hold of me. *Yes! It's turned off!* This time I didn't rely on my eyes, but wrapped up the cord and put it on the counter. I touched the end of the cord. I touched the curling iron itself. Cold. I put it down. Then I picked it up and went through the whole ritual again. And again. And again . . . and again. I was exhausted. I felt as if I couldn't believe what I was seeing, what I knew to be true. I placed my hand over the outlet, trying to make my body believe what my mind wouldn't.

Gary agreed to see me on very short notice. I'd been so sure that I would be different, that I wouldn't need special favors, that I wouldn't ever need to ask for help between appointments. As soon as I got to his office, he could see that I was upset. He helped me take several long breaths before I launched into some of what had been tormenting me. Perhaps it was because I'd been unable to see him for several weeks, or perhaps it was because I'd ventured into the boxes while he was away, or . . . well, perhaps I was simply going nuts. Who knew?

When we talked about my past up to this point, details I provided him were sketchy and uncomfortable. When relating any information, my face grew hot and flushed, and I felt what I can only describe as shame. I glanced anxiously at the clock, aching for the hour to be up. Finally, at one of our visits not long ago, Gary simply turned the clock away from me. Problem solved. We'd spent a great deal of time together . . . more than enough for him to become bored. But he gently and patiently relaxed my resistance and never pushed me to talk about anything I didn't want to.

The road I'd taken wasn't linear but circuitous. I'd paused, lately, in my therapy, to take a breath. Gary respected that, but didn't allow lingering sightseeing on my side trips. My detours were many, but with his perceptive attention, even they became brilliant teachers.

I knew that all wouldn't be revealed in the first session, nor the fifth, nor even the twentieth. There were weeks when I had nothing new to contribute, or was simply tired and felt as if I was wasting both our time and my money. These periods too, though, served as teachers. Was I denying pertinent feelings? Repressing emotions too close to the surface? In most cases, yes. It was with Gary's attentive, empathic nature that I was able to finally recognize and attach meaning to these periods as well.

For the first time since I'd started seeing Gary, though, I cared more about what I had to say than what he thought about me. I needed to get what I had in my head, out. Out into the air. Out where it could reach someone else's ears. Out where I could get some help. My words now were for me, not him.

So I related the story from the beginning, with as much detail and courage as I could gather. Of course, not all the details that I'm relating here were told that first day, but rather in fits and starts throughout our time together. It was the first time I took Gary into the house with me, through my words and memories. I remember telling him that I had a scream, deep down inside me, that was trying to come out. A scream for help . . .

It was a Thursday, 4:30 by the time I got to the bus stop. And I'll never forget the date, ever. June 17, 1976. The air was sweet and clear; San Francisco was at its most beautiful. The fog hung low until late morning this time of year and returned in early evening, carpeting the city in a delicate shroud.

A sudden, violent push against my back forced me into the bushes on my hands and knees, scraping my cheek and tearing my tights. The pain in my knees was tremendous, and I felt angry that I'd been hit. I turned my head around, glimpsing the face of a man I didn't recognize as he wrapped my long hair around his hand. He stood upright, pulling me to my feet, twisting my arm around my back. My hands grasped the air in front of me for my purse and the book I'd been reading while waiting for the bus.

We rushed across the street as he scolded me, my feet reaching for the ground. He was screaming obscenities and speaking to me as if we knew each other. "How could you do this to me? I told you last time that I was going to find out." On and on. I thought for a moment that he had me confused with someone else until I noticed a man on the street turn away upon seeing us. I panicked. He intended to give the impression that I was his girlfriend or wife so that no one would get involved. His words became noise . . . static in my brain. My head was pounding so loudly I couldn't hear a word.

He motioned to a house across the street, and was saying something. I tried to nod, but he had such a tight grip on my hair that my head wouldn't move. I tried to cry out but produced nothing. We were getting closer to the house. Terror kept my voice locked inside me. He was moving me. Controlling me. My feet barely touched the pavement. He hurried up the steps in front of me, kicking the front door open and dragging me inside.

Still holding my hair, he turned me around to face him. My eyes, or maybe my brain, seemed to take a quick inventory of him without my even realizing what was happening. He was tall . . . maybe 6'2" or 6'3" and had curly blond hair to his shoulders. His green eyes were bizarre. They paralyzed me; they locked onto mine and chilled me the entire length of my body. I saw an angry, stabbing hate in his eyes, and I knew he was going to hurt me.

He was wearing a large, cream-colored sweater. The sleeves hung long on his arms, even though he was tall. He had some kind of shirt on underneath, like a jean shirt. I remember seeing blue underneath the round collar of the sweater. He was wearing jeans, and I remember thinking they were more straight than bell bottom. His shoes were made of leather, and had a seam up the front. All these impressions came to me in an instant.

His hands were on my shoulders as he looked down at me. I expected him to say something, then I felt myself flying backward, experiencing this weird sensation as he moved further from me, his eyes still locked onto mine. My arms flailed behind me trying to find the floor, but my butt hit first, then my elbows, then my head banged against the hardwood floor, knocking me out.

I woke hours later lying on a thin mattress on the floor. My senses were overwhelmed, but I oriented myself quickly and remembered where I was ... what had taken place. The feeling of being in a nightmare flooded me. It was quiet in the room and dark now. My eyes didn't want to adjust. I tried to focus on things in the room. I was strangely ... acutely aware. Renovation was taking place in the house. A noxious mixture of fresh paint and stain used to refinish hardwood floors filled my head, making it ache. I didn't hear him around me, which only served to make me more anxious.

There was no furniture in the room except the mattress I was lying on and an unlighted lamp without a shade in the corner. The mattress was old, blue and white striped, and thin ... scrawny enough to feel the floor underneath. A rancid smell from beneath my face as I turned — stains, sweat, and dirt mixed together — overtook the other odors in the house, making me nauseous.

Heavy, tasseled shades covered the bay windows, and it was darker now than before. Sounds were different. There was a kitchen to my right and a pass-through above me, the barrel of a small handgun visible over the edge of the counter.

Another wave of panic washed over me and, while it was not cold in the house, I trembled uncontrollably. My fear was palpable; my dread, I'm quite sure, one could smell. I tried to calm myself as one would if a dangerous animal was near.

Except for a light shining through the frosted windows in the back of the kitchen, there was no other light. I saw him out of the corner of my eye at the same time he noticed me move. I pretended to be still, but it was too late. In a moment, he was on top of me, struggling to push my legs apart and get inside me. I froze. Paralyzed, my heart raced; drawing a breath was nearly impossible, I was so petrified.

His body was hot, almost burning, but his hands were like ice, rough and violent and tearing into my flesh. He had tied my hands in front of me before I woke, and had taken off my underpants and tights. I'd worn a jean skirt with snaps down the front, sort of country-looking, and a jean blouse. Only one snap was still fastened, and he'd unbuttoned my blouse and had opened it to my sides. It seems odd, but I remember thinking about my new coat, a dark green London Fog that I'd saved months for, and how it was getting dirty on this mattress. It was hanging off my shoulder on one side, and completely off on the other side.

My hands were bleeding from cuts he'd made while tying me up, and the blood dripped onto my stomach. The skin on my arm against my stomach felt familiar and warm, a contrast to his cold hands. His skin felt strange against mine. He lay on top of me with nothing on, his penis against my leg, trying to push himself inside me. It wasn't hard enough to get inside, so he pushed his fingers in instead.

The muscles in my thighs ached. Instead of yielding to his demand to spread my legs, I squeezed them tighter together. He continued to struggle, trying to push himself inside me. I felt as if I was an animal to him, as if I was no longer human . . . just a receptacle. I was trapped. I ached to get out from underneath his body, but couldn't get any leverage. Pushing my head against his shoulder, I tried to get up. Words escaped from my mouth with no connection to my head. I heard pleading . . . begging. It sounded like my voice, yet I was horrified to realize that it was only in my head. Only a whisper . . . a moan . . . escaped.

My fear of him was primal. Deep. I didn't understand, couldn't comprehend the words he was saying. They ran together and fell on my ears like gibberish. Was I going crazy? Why couldn't I understand? Follow his directions? My thoughts bounced off the inside of my brain. A massive scream rising inside me stopped short. He struggled again to pry my legs apart, and I struggled just as hard to keep them together. My thigh muscles burned, the effort was so intense.

His face was close to mine; he was pushing his tongue in my mouth, his hands pulling at me. My breath quickened, turned into panting . . . one of his hands between my legs, the other holding my jaw, forcing me to face him, to stop twisting.

He was furious with me and becoming more forceful. He backed up and sat on his knees between my legs, bringing his left hand back. I knew I was going to be hit, but when his fist finally slammed straight into my chin, I felt nothing at first. I was . . . overwhelmed. Shocked at the force with which he hit me, dazed by my own lack of power over his strength. This couldn't be happening to me.

I took a deep breath, sucking in some of the blood that had already begun to flow. My tongue instinctively took inventory. My teeth were holding on with thin threads, so I worked them around and stood them up, pushing against them with my tongue on the inside and keeping my lip stiff. Cut and bleeding, my lip swelled right away. I turned my face to the left and spit blood onto the mattress, choking on some that ran down my throat. I brought my head back around and his fist slammed again into my face, this time into the right side of my jaw. I knew it was broken; the sound of my bone breaking sickened me.

My eyes stopped focusing as the pain of his punches finally reached me. He kept pounding my body . . . legs . . . chest . . . stomach . . . face . . . breathing was difficult, becoming impossible. Anticipation of where his fist would land next was hopeless, and agonizing when it finally made contact with my body.

His words brought me around. Imploring me, then threatening me to give him what he wanted. I was confused and angry. It was not I who was hurting him. He was in control. He asked me again and again why I was so fucking tight, spitting the words from his mouth to degrade me. I managed to whisper that I'd never been with a man.

Telling the truth was a mistake, serving only to make him more excited. His physical assault was constant; his verbal description of what he was going to do to me was malicious and grotesque. I heard only words . . . disconnected from any meaning . . . they didn't fall together in sentences . . . "fucking cunt . . . you'll pay . . . never leaving me . . . fucking bitch." Exhaustion engulfed me. I was consumed with the simple act of trying to anticipate. No resistance met him when he spread my legs this time; my muscles gave way under his force.

Shock registered on his face when he heard the muted, animal sounds that escaped me. He had betrayed me. I'd anticipated him trying to penetrate me with his penis again, and so had surrendered. Instead, he pushed something sharp inside me, thrusting it in hard until it stopped, then pulling it out again. Over and over, he repeated the motion, making me squirm on the thin mattress. Intense cramps in my back added to his punishment of me; no matter how I tried, I couldn't make the pain stop.

Instinctively, I tried to grasp at the object he was violating me with, but I couldn't grab hold with my hands tied. My fingers grasped and clawed, but I felt nothing but his cold hands. Calloused hands, unaffected by the pain my fingernails must have made. He pushed against something terribly sensitive, making my back arch in agony, bringing a soft, deep, black sleep.

When I came to, my legs were splayed apart like a doll. He was still pushing something inside me, and my passing out had allowed him to get still further in. Feverish, I fought the feeling of being sick. I was repulsed to see him reach between my legs and smear some of my blood on both our stomachs and thighs.

I couldn't think straight. Everything was wrong. Upside down. It was Thursday; I needed to be at Elaine's house. I needed my life back. The urge to grab him with both hands and dig my fingernails deep into his flesh was overwhelming. I wanted to make him bleed and suffer. I wanted to make him scream in pain. I wanted to make him stop, but I could do none of it. My entire body was seized with dread. Terror pulled at my insides; I was so frightened to do something which might make him more angry still.

My face was horribly swollen, and my breathing had become raspy and labored. Blood trickled down the back of my throat. Lying on my back became unmanageable. Raising my hands to him, with the words barely slipping between my lips, I pleaded with him to untie me. To my surprise, he did. I raised my hands toward him again but couldn't reach his body. He had seen my hands reaching for him, and backed away, his long arms still sufficient for tearing into me. I held onto the sides of the mattress and brought them up to enfold me while he continued. A fleeting thought ... perhaps if I brought the sides in tight enough, I could slip through his grip. I knew, of course, that I could not. It felt good to have something to hold on to, though. To push in to.

The cramps in my back returned more intensely; he was giving me so little room for movement. So tight. He grew tired and started to pull out whatever he had inside me. I could sense what he was about to do, and grew restless. Squirming, I wanted it out of me. Now. And I needed to see what he was abusing me with.

The pain of removing the object was prolonged ... it took a lifetime to get it out of me. I wanted it out. I wanted him out. I wanted out of this house. I brought my legs up and rolled onto my right side, holding my stomach after he removed it. The void left me raw. My face swollen and excruciating, he left me lying there like an animal along the road. I felt blood rush out of me and tears well up in my eyes and roll down my cheeks, pooling beneath me on the mattress. I was desperately, horribly alone.

Exhausted, he left me alone and fell against the wall toward my feet. I was no longer his priority, for the time being. The respite was welcome, but left me anxious and extremely distressed, for it gave me time to anticipate his next actions. There was a part of me that wished to just get it all over with ... whatever he had in mind. I ached to move but couldn't, so I lay on my side holding my stomach, just as he left me. Looking at him was horrid ... nauseating, but I couldn't look elsewhere. My head, my body, didn't respond as I wanted them to. I didn't move a muscle. In my mind, I rose from the mattress, picked up my raincoat, and walked to the door; but in reality, I was frozen in place.

A paralysis that began with my feet worked its way up my legs into my thighs, into my stomach ... panic took hold of me, squeezing my chest tight. I was terrified. What would happen if the paralysis hit my throat, my breathing, my swallowing? Would my breath just simply stop? Was this house where I was going to die? What was happening to me? I couldn't move to save my life.

He was freebasing cocaine. I knew then that his hostility, his anger, was only going to escalate. The smoke was heavy in the room. I fought to keep myself together. I had to remain coherent in order to get out of the house, but the sweet aroma of the cocaine swirled around my head, making me dizzy and light-headed. Desperate to surrender to the deep sleep it might bring, I was frightened nonetheless to lose more control. My eyes felt heavy; opening and closing them became a major undertaking. I was unsure whether it was from the effects of the cocaine or what he had put me through. Each time they closed, I felt an overwhelming urge to keep them closed, to surrender, to leave. My body, my mind, were both in shock.

Letters appeared in front of my eyes, at first just floating in space. I tried to make words of them. I tried so desperately to concentrate, to see the words the letters were forming. Vibrating, spinning letters, huge letters . . . while I focused on them, I was unable to focus on him, on what was happening to me, on my injuries.

Finally the letters slowed and stopped spinning. I was able to right them in my mind, to strip away the garish colors and the wild patterns that filled them, surrounded them. Go over them again to make them the same size. Go over them again to line them up. Go over them again to put them in proper order. My mind was consumed with my work. I had begun reading The Prophet the week before, and was memorizing the splendid words; their beauty so impressed me. My heart ached realizing that the specially bound copy I had saved to buy was outside in the bushes. Warm tears moved down my cheeks. Outside . . . outside . . .

Striving to recall what Gibran had written, to sort them out, I saw before me the actual words on the page. I struggled harder to remember them, and intently worked at putting them in the right order. He spoke of houses. Houses like this. One word came. Then another. The effort was intense and exhausting, but I had to make the words come. I was depleting my resources . . . I knew that . . . but I couldn't stop.

Then those words that I grasped turned brilliant in color and started to wave and pulsate. They ran together and then backed away from each other, taking on a life of their own. Patterns filled my mind again with colors and shapes and feelings and sizes and fonts and . . . then another word. Like a gift . . . another word. Then another until I had a full passage. The tiny trickle of tears down my face turned into wracking sobs. I couldn't stop. My tears were burning my cheeks.

Houses and fastened doors. My head felt heavy and sore. I looked to my right and saw him rise onto his knees. The blackness of the room seemed to make his skin look even *more white. I could see his face more clearly now but didn't feel . . . anything . . . anything at all. I drew a breath, smelling the blood on my lips. I'd forgotten to breathe.*

Fastened doors. Doors that keep you in. I struggled hard to remember. Remember. Remember my books . . . my dog . . . my parents . . . my bed . . . my home. Remember. Like a gift, more of his text came back to me.

" . . . hands . . . silken . . ." The text floated from my grasp. Pulsating, spinning in my head, the words grew large and blood red, then creamy and soft, almost translucent. Dignity. He spoke of it, I know, yet I couldn't reach it. I couldn't reach the words no matter how I tried. He was stealing my dignity, this man. This animal. I needed words now. Comforting words. Words that would make me know I was going to get out of this house and back into my life.

These words came to me, but not as you see them here. They took a long time . . . a long, long time to form. One word laid upon the other. You shall not be trapped. Nor tamed. The words, the letters, the fonts, the sizes, the paper the soft, sweet color of vanilla ice cream, all of it swirled around my head. The gentle smell of the trees from which the paper was made. I felt as if in a dream. Walking farther and farther out of my body. I watched him as if looking at him would make him go away. Make all this go away . . . as if it would erase all of this.

Being outside myself brought a . . . surrender, I suppose, of sorts. If I was no longer in my body, then I couldn't be hurt. A strange, eerie calm came over me . . . not like when one is relaxing, of course. More like resolve. Inexplicable, I suppose, the feeling that didn't come from within, but rather surrounded my being. I felt as if I had to comprehend something incomprehensible in order to survive. I had to stop asking "why" at that moment. Later, I could return to questions, but for now . . .

I noticed parts of his body for the first time. He didn't look like a rapist. He didn't look like the monster he was. I became furious. He was supposed to look like the monster he was; otherwise, how could I know what he was? As he slumped against the wall, he looked like any other guy on the street. My mind, my body, my blood, bones, nerves . . . everything inside me was filled with rage. I fought losing myself. Time stood still. I closed my eyes.

I suppose a deep, soft sleep overtook me, as it was much later than it had been. The streets were quiet . . . sounds were muffled like they are when the fog lowers into the crevices of the buildings and descends like cat's paws onto their roofs. This time of night always gave me comfort and solace. Innately, I knew that I would never experience this time of night with the innocence I once knew. Sounds that had comforted before, that I hadn't even fully heard, were now alarmingly absent. Only after they were missing had I noticed them fully: sounds of the family in the apartment in the back, sounds of TV shows.

Because it was quieter outside, I knew that I was more alone with him. Normal, everyday life was going on all around me, but I was no longer part of it. The person I was when I awoke that morning no longer existed. Tremendous, overwhelming loss devoured me. Now there was only silence except for a foghorn, moaning long and low in the distance. Only emptiness in my heart. No one would hear me, even if I gathered the courage to cry out. I clutched the mattress tightly.

The pain throughout my body was intense. I had several moments, perhaps longer, before he woke as well. His head had slumped against his chest as he slept; one leg was bent and the other stretched out in front of him. His penis lay innocuously against his thigh. Not the threat it had been earlier, but it ... he ... could come to life at any time. An overwhelming awareness of his power and my lack of it threw me into despair. How was I going to get out of this house?

I was so lost in myself, I barely realized that he'd awakened and was speaking to me again. His tone had changed. Apologetic almost, he started a diatribe. This isn't what he wanted to do, he explained. He didn't want to hurt me, honestly. His eyes implored me for understanding of what he had to do. Nauseated, anger engulfed me. How dare he ask for understanding of what he did ... of what he was still doing to me. He declared his compassion for my plight; a cruel joke. Green eyes, dilated nearly fully, eclipsed by large, black pupils, stared back at me as he stabbed me with his words.

Moody, though, his professed compassion for me didn't last. Questions he asked of me went unanswered. Statements he made passed over me without reaction. I was dead inside. He met my reticence, my rebellion, with more hostility, telling me that I was even more beautiful when wracking pain crossed my face, like before. Still on my side, I lay staring at him. We were at a stalemate. We both understood that he had the power in the room. We both knew he could force me to do what he wanted.

I knew then that he intended to make me experience even more horror that night. Our dance was over, and he was ready once again.

He retied my hands. The candle sitting atop the pass-through flickered each time he slumped against the wall. Terrified that it would fall on the mattress and that I would be burned alive, it kept me mesmerized. He noticed me looking up ... a cue to begin again.

When he finished berating me for looking where I shouldn't have, for being "bad," for being a worthless whore, he pushed me onto my back, spread my legs, and moved in toward me. Reaching up for the candle, he poured the melted wax pooled in the hollow of the candle over my chest. Intense, excruciating pain overtook me. The wax fell onto my breast near my nipple and rolled down into the center of my chest, blistering my skin as it flowed down. Pulling my hair back and baring my throat to his mouth, he bit into my neck and growled into my ear that I was going to wish I was dead. I whispered that I already did.

This time he was able to penetrate me. Wanting him to get inside me, to get what he needed so he'd get off me and leave me alone, so he'd let me go home and take care of myself, or so he'd leave me to die, became my goal. Something other than this torture. He slammed into me again and again, but still could not ejaculate. My hands were tied in front of me; every movement was sheer agony. I felt my skin pull on my bones, he was so rough. He made sounds ... grunts more like an animal than a human being as we settled into a sick, disgusting conspiracy in which we both had the same goal: for him to come.

After an excruciatingly long time, he reached his frustration point and pushed me onto my left side. He stood up and kicked me in the back, then moved in front of me and knelt down. Reaching around my head, he pulled me to him, trying to push his penis into my mouth. Swollen, broken, bruised ... it didn't matter to him. He wanted only to humiliate me. I couldn't help choking, and pulled back. Blood flowed anew from my teeth and jaw; his movements had intensified the pain, upset the delicate balance that I had tried to maintain in my mouth. My jaw was broken, so physically accommodating him inside my mouth was impossible. The pain was too great. I pushed my hands, still tied, against his thighs and abdomen. The thought of him coming in my mouth was repulsive.

I made resolutions with myself nearly minute by minute. If I made it through the next ten minutes ... if I made it through the next fifteen minutes ...

He tested my limits for enduring pain. He didn't want sex from me, but defilement. He was enraged that I couldn't take him in my mouth, and again filled me with anxiety as he fell against the wall. I rolled onto my back, feeling tremendous pressure in my bladder; the need to urinate had become urgent. I pressed my pelvis into the mattress and brought my legs closer together to try and calm myself, to stop shaking as that was making it worse. When that only intensified the feeling, I brought my hands down and pushed against my lower abdomen. I couldn't afford further humiliation. It became a stubborn show of preventing him from seeing what he was doing to me.

I whispered that I had to go to the bathroom, trying to sound calm as I said it, as though it were not as pressing as it truly was. I could go, he told me, pointing the way.

But he wouldn't untie my hands. A small victory. I struggled to stand, but it was impossible to walk. Even if he untied my hands, I hadn't the strength, so I crawled the twenty or so feet to the bathroom on my knees and the outsides of my hands, dragging my clothes behind me. I was shivering, afraid I wouldn't make it. I waited for him to grab me at any moment from behind and drag me back to the mattress. I didn't feel his hands on my body, so I kept moving slowly along the floor, afraid to look back at him. After about twenty minutes of feeling each wood grain of the hardwood floor, of slowly, methodically putting the outside of my hands down onto the cold floor, then one knee, then the other, and then starting all over again, I reached the bathroom.

I don't remember returning to the front room, or even having gone to the bathroom, but I was back on the mattress when I awoke. Just the top snap of my jean skirt was fastened, keeping my skirt around me. My eyes burned, and my face was flush. This wasn't ending. I was lost, and no one knew where I was or what was happening to me. No one was going to rescue me.

He clawed at me again, trying to open my legs, yelling at me to spread them. I couldn't open my mouth enough to say that I was trying. He knelt between my legs and grabbed me by my ankles. He drew me toward him, pulling me up by my hips. Gripped by fear, I knew he was going to sodomize me.

He turned me over, crushing the right side of face into the mattress, laying me against my jaw. I twisted my head down and to the right and brought it back around to lie on the left side of my face. My hands were still tied in front of me, so my head was at an angle again. I couldn't catch my breath. I begged him not to do this and to untie my hands, stretching my mouth as much as I could to make myself heard. My jaw bones ground together. I became disoriented again and felt as if I would pass out, but was finally able to get a little more than a whisper out of my mouth.

He reached underneath me and untied my hands, stuffing the blood-soaked cloth into my mouth. Shaking, I kept swallowing to keep from becoming sick. He had both my hands in his, still behind my back, making it impossible to get any leverage. It seemed like forever. I kept sucking in air, and along with it, dirt and my blood on the cloth. No air escaped from me. I stopped resisting. My whole body engaged in trying to get air inside my lungs. A strange sensation of my muscles going limp and soft ... of feeling like a puppet in his hands ... thoughts ran through my mind. Just go ahead, do it, it doesn't matter. This is what it feels like to die. To grow soft and feel your muscles relaxing their grip on life. To surrender.

Suddenly he grew tired and let my hands go. The desire to take another breath was stronger than the inviting blackness and, as soon as he released my hands, I yanked the cloth from my mouth.

He pulled my skirt up around my waist and sodomized me without any preliminaries. The pain was vicious and raw. He kept pushing, breaking me in two, chastising me for the blood running down the inside of my thighs. Trying to hold on . . . to breathe deeply; animal grunts escaped from deep inside me. He told me he was going to rip me in two.

Astounded, I felt myself just . . . flow out of my body. Ever so softly, in sharp contrast to his hard, vicious movements, mine, in moving outside myself, were softened and gradual. I moved to a corner in the room and watched what was happening to me. The disorientation was excruciating, the confusion too much to bear. Disconnection from the girl lying on the mattress left me with the feeling of having abandoned her, as if she were truly all alone.

I moved my body to accommodate the pain, but became numb. Completely motionless. I shifted between looking outside my eyes and being outside my body. Alarmed at what was happening to me, it all became too much. I had to leave my body in order to remain sane. Pushing against him, I rose up on my hands and knees. I was relieved to be able to breathe again. Because he penetrated me anally, though, when I finally got to my knees, I felt a tremendous bolt of pain shoot up my back. He continued for a long time, slamming his penis into me, the front of his thighs shoving against the back of mine.

He taunted me, threatening to go deeper inside. A blinding anger overtook me and burned my insides. My muscles closed in around him, as much in rage as in pain. I reached out in front of the mattress to the hardwood floor. Hard and real, it was something I could touch, something to grab onto. My fingers dug into the floor. Panic-stricken, I was inside my body again. An unsettled, disconcerted feeling overwhelmed me, at how I was able to experience this but be looking at myself at the same time. Frightened of him, I was even more terrified of what was happening to me. I was sure he was driving me insane.

He pulled me toward him with such a ferocious jerk that my hands came up off the floor and then back down again with a thud. I clawed at the floor, stretching my fingers in front of me, frantically trying to get away from him. My hands were surreal to me. Disembodied and disconnected from my arms, I saw them in front of me as if they were not mine. I didn't recognize them. At one point they looked opaque, as if I could see the blood flowing through them and see the bones and nerves. Pieces of the floor mixed with blood underneath my fingernails.

He came inside me with furious energy, convulsing again and again. He pushed against me, holding onto my hips, bringing them toward him. Pulling out of me finally didn't bring the measure of relief I needed. The torment was beyond words. He fell against the wall and passed out almost immediately.

Without his hands supporting my hips, I dropped to my stomach, then onto my right side on the mattress, unable to move. I was exhausted and felt broken in two. My energy, my fight, was gone. All I could do was lie there motionless and stare out of my eyes. I noticed the wall before me, the small strokes a brush had made on the newly painted surface and the way it intersected with the ornate baseboard. How very intricate and pretty, I remember thinking. A deep, black sleep came over me.

When I awoke, the only sound in the room was my heart beating loudly in my ears and a pounding in my throat. I didn't move a muscle. I was afraid he would hear, and drew a deep breath in order to calm myself. Getting as much air into my lungs as possible, like when one goes under water and doesn't know when they'll be able to breathe again, my breathing became short and barely audible.

It was difficult, but I kept my eyes closed when I heard him stir. I opened my eyes when I thought I heard him leave the room. He moved to the kitchen and stayed there quite some time, and I remember him saying something to me, but I don't recall what it was. I was frozen in place.

He came back and called me a fucking whore. He bent toward me and told me to open my eyes and make myself come. I shook my head and pointed to my face. I whispered that I might be sick, and he became even more angry. He took the gun from the pass-through to the kitchen and put it under my chin, threatening to blow my face off if I didn't make myself come.

I disconnected completely from him again . . . the house . . . the pain . . . myself . . . and escaped. I was gentle with myself. I knew that my life depended on my being able to do this, and so did what he demanded. Still angry with me, he accused me of faking it and threatened me, telling me to continue. I couldn't. I was exhausted. His hand came down hard on my neck, his fingers squeezing hard into my throat. Vile admonitions poured from him, but the pressure against my neck and chest made him appear far away and hard to understand. I moved in slow motion. Bringing my hands up to his, I dug hard into his flesh and felt his blood seep onto my hand and moisten my palms.

His sudden, spastic movement frightened me. He moved the gun to my cheek and, without hesitation, pulled the trigger. My breath . . . my heart stopped. Our eyes locked as we waited for the bullet to rip into my face. To blow my head apart. The next second felt like a lifetime of agony; my entire life had come to this house, this man, this rape . . . this moment.

No sound. I'd expected to hear a thunderous blast rip through my head, but there was no sound. He pulled back from me and stood emptying the bullets into his hand, counting them. One . . . two . . . three . . . four . . . five . . . A vicious, cruel laugh erupted from him as he flung the gun and the bullets onto the counter in the kitchen. I was sorry there were not six.

My eyes locked onto his again as he came toward me. I remember making a mental note that he was left-handed. He had to be; he'd hit the right side of my jaw, and then he had the gun in his left hand just now. He was left-handed; I remember saying it over and over so I could tell the police . . .

My energy drained from me, and I felt as if I were dying. I had no further resources. No fantasies of escape. No hope. Numbing nothingness overtook me. He fell down upon me again and pushed himself inside me. We were not there for me; we were there for him. I was no longer a human being, but a piece of flesh. He knew it and I knew it. His penis reached up high into my belly. He ejaculated, arching his back and holding tightly onto me. A moment later, he started again and then again, ejaculating each time. My eyes stared straight into his. He turned his face away from me and continued violating me. My agony became hopelessness. I thought his was the last face I would ever see.

The next moments are a blur. I have distorted, chaotic images of this period and wish, in a way, that I could recall it more clearly . . . but then am grateful that I cannot. I recall the feeling of numbness in my body and how my skin moved over my bones with each thrust he made inside me, and I remember how I had a thought that it felt like my skin was a dress that was a couple of sizes too big. It was moving so much over my bones.

And I have a remembrance of light shining ever so softly along the edges of the shades, not as if the sun was shining, but that it was light out. I remember small passages from songs coming from nearby apartments where people were getting ready for work or school. " . . . good morning, starshine . . . " and later — I'm not sure how much later — the same words, and the same words again. I remember wondering if I was really hearing them so many times, or had they played that song on all the stations. Or maybe, I thought, I was going crazy.

I remember him slumped against the wall, his head in an agonizing, unreal position.

And I remember sliding along the floor somehow, making my way toward the door. I wasn't on my hands and knees, but I had my knees underneath me and was sitting on them, bending forward, pulling myself along on the outsides of my arms. I remember moving the slightest amount, then being very still, waiting for him to grab me from behind, then moving again, the slightest amount, then being very still, waiting for him to grab me from behind. And on and on. My coat and skirt dragged behind me. I remember them pulling each time I moved forward.

All I have of actually leaving the coffin he'd made out of the house is a faint perception, or maybe just a sense of tremendous safety having passed the threshold. I don't know, can't remember, if awareness of the safety of leaving was with me at that moment, or if it came later.

My next recollection is of a man stopping me on the street, grabbing me by the shoulders, asking if I was okay. Any feeling of safety and relief that I'd gotten out of the house had dissipated by that point, and I knew I had to make it home. Terrified to look behind me, I frantically nodded. Please don't hold me back . . . don't touch me, I wanted to say. I have to get home. And he let me go.

The look on the man's face torments me even now as my shattered, bloody face reflected in his expression. He looked relieved to let me go, as if he had fulfilled his obligation by asking. I despise him for not doing what was right. Had he helped me, perhaps taken me someplace where I would be safe, I could have reported the rape right away and gotten the medical help I needed. But I was in no position to ask. And he was in no position to provide what I needed.

My contact with him woke me from the daze I was in, making me aware of my surroundings. I had come the four blocks or so from the rapist's house, and was nearly home. It was becoming light; people were congregating at the bus stops along Van Ness, ready to go to work. Everyday life was happening around me again, only this morning I was removed. I didn't understand the magnitude of what had happened yet. I could scarcely believe I had been in his house overnight. It had seemed like an eternity. The person I was yesterday, was dead.

I finally made it home . . . bleeding and raw. I found myself standing in my bathtub. I'd turned on the shower. I don't recall how I got home exactly, or even how long I'd been standing there. It had to be . . . 9:00 or 10:00 a.m. I no longer heard sounds of people leaving for work. No sounds at all, in fact, except for my heart pounding in my ears. Words from the same book I'd been reading that came to me during the rape, again invaded my thoughts . . . chaining themselves together . . .

slowly forming sentences I'd meticulously memorized not so long ago, but a lifetime away. I tried to make sense of what happened but it was too soon. Words came to me, but something was terribly wrong. Instead of my voice, I heard that of the man raping me, his words scorching my ears.

The words ran through my head ... louder and louder still ... until I felt as if I would go mad; I just wanted them to stop. I wanted to be anywhere else, anyone else than who I was at that moment. The fear that gripped me tight around the neck like a noose stayed with me. Stays with me still. The water was scalding, but still not hot enough. It would, I hoped, burn the memory of the man from me. The steam would peel the skin from where he'd touched me. He had changed my life forever.

As in the rapist's house, time lost meaning. Leaning my hands against the tile, I shifted my weight from one foot to the other, and back. I felt no ... emotions ... just a numbness that seeped through my flesh into my bones. If only I could feel something. What was wrong with me? Why couldn't I feel anything? I didn't want to believe any of this had happened.

I stared straight ahead at the wall of the shower until a droplet of water demanded my attention. Focusing intently, I watched as it mapped a path along a band of grout ... and on along each tile until it plunged ever so softly from the faucet to join the blood and water pooling in the tub around my feet. It seemed that I watched hundreds and hundreds of these tiny droplets fall to their demise, though I'm not sure how long, in fact, I stood there watching. Well into my study, it dawned on me that it was my blood that I was watching pool around my feel and swirl into the drain. How much could I lose, I wondered, without passing out ... without dying? My hair, matted and wet, came out in clumps when I pushed it back from my face.

Each small drop of water blistered my skin where it landed. My whole body ached. My hands fell to my sides. Looking down, I bent my elbows and brought my palms up, turning them over and back again. They seemed foreign to me. It seemed the only places on my body that didn't have a bruise, a cut, a burn, were on the palms of my hands and my knees. I felt along my sides, taking an inventory of my injuries. My hands became my eyes. I couldn't bring myself to look at what he had done, but I knew I had to determine how badly I was hurt. My breasts were incredibly tender, and while I was able to feel my left breast with my hand, feeling my right was excruciating. The image of him pouring candle wax onto me flooded over me. I felt the pain much more intensely in the shower than I had in his house.

My hands moved down along my stomach and then further down. I imagined that I must look like a bruised peach, but still could not look. I brought my hand along my hips and then inside me ... it was covered in blood. Disbelief ... shock ... took hold. He'd violated me in the most intimate ways. The simplest movements were piercingly painful. My thigh muscles burned and grew heavy; everything became tired, and I started shivering. My legs betrayed me. My knees buckled, but I didn't make an effort to catch myself, and slowly floated to the floor of the bathtub in unbelievable pain. Sitting was impossible, so I knelt on the floor as in prayer. The irony wasn't lost on me. I brought myself onto my hands and knees and stayed that way, with my head down, just ... being still ... with the water beating against my back for hours. Vulnerable and open and violated.

As comforting as the shower had been at first, it became unbearably irritating. Dizzy and suddenly nauseous, I had to get out. My muscles had stiffened and were no longer cooperating with me, so I crawled up and over the side of the tub and lay down on my side on the bathmat, holding my stomach. Fear gripped me once again as memories of what had happened overwhelmed me. The thought that perhaps the rapist had followed me and knew where I lived seized my thoughts. Perhaps he's in my apartment at this moment ... perhaps he's outside the bathroom door, waiting for me ... perhaps ... perhaps he's waiting for me in my bed. Wait ... where are my keys? How had I gotten in? I didn't ... couldn't ... remember.

Afraid to move, I lay there forever. Motionless. Breathless. Terrified to make a sound. Afraid to even towel myself off for fear of him hearing me. I knew if he was out there waiting for me; surely he would hear the relentless, deafening pounding of my heart. Nausea gripped my stomach when, without warning, I became violently sick. Fluids poured from me as my body tried to purge the brutality that the man had put me through.

I knew I had to get help. A lot of time had passed while I was on the floor in the bathroom, and I couldn't lie there any longer. I spent a great deal of time simply planning the task of cleaning up. Slowly, painstakingly, I began my work. My movements were minute; I so feared throwing up again. Each time I opened my mouth, my bones ground together, doing further damage. Because of having been sodomized, sitting up was impossible, and a cut on my right hip made leaning to that side unbearable. Each movement became a new way in which to relate to my body, a new way I had to learn in order to even stand up. Each movement was a discovery of an injury.

I made a move. My energy drained from my body, and I grew dizzy; all I wanted was to lie back and rest, but I forced myself to sit and calm the feeling so that I could continue. Five minutes stretched into ten, and then fifteen without another movement.

Then, when my stomach and head felt calmer, another movement. Twenty minutes this time. Another movement. Ten minutes passed. Another movement and another, until I had rolled up the bathmat and cleaned up the blood and vomit and urine on the floor.

After cleaning up the bathroom, I gathered my courage and slowly, painfully made my way out into the hallway, grimacing with each step. The rapist wasn't in the apartment, but on the floor in front of my bedroom door were my clothes in a pile. The clothes I'd put on yesterday morning. The clothes I was raped in. They were bloody and torn and lifeless. What a strange way to describe them . . . to describe me . . .

I didn't want to look at them, or touch them, but I couldn't have them in my home. I scooped them up in my arms and painfully walked to the kitchen door. Outside was a trash chute leading to an incinerator. I opened the door and threw the clothes . . . the evidence . . . in. It wasn't until I was back in my apartment that I realized I had no clothes on.

I put on a pair of jeans and a clean tee shirt and fell onto my bed. I felt swollen and sore, and my jeans barely fit. But I needed to get to the dentist soon. It was already 4:30. Most of the day had been spent lying in the shower, lying on the bathmat, and cleaning up the bathroom, but I knew I was simply prolonging my agony. I looked around my bedroom. I had tried to brighten the cramped little room with brilliant yellow and soft lavender flowers, and I had just refinished a small chest of drawers that I bought for $10. Small, delicate daffodils on an ivy wound their way up, reaching toward the flowers in the vase on top and then falling back down, it seemed, onto the floor. And on the walls, posters of kitties and butterflies and sweet sayings designed to help me make it through the difficulties, the boredom, the pain that everyone feels at one time or another. A necklace that Rob had given me hung over the edge of the mirror above the dresser. I hadn't realized until that moment that I hadn't heard from him yet that day. Odd. Records propped against the wall next to a record player . . . It was the bedroom, I realized, of an innocent, young girl, a virgin. My life would never be the same.

I called my dentist, sort of gurgling into the phone when I reached the nurse. Accident . . . need to see him right away . . . He had time for me if I came now, she said, so I grabbed my keys and wallet and caught a bus. I avoided looks. I knew my face was deeply bruised, and I still had my mouth tightly closed in order to save my front teeth. Just get me there, I thought. Just get me there so I can get back.

Being outside again felt alien. The pain in my jaw alone propelled me to his office. I felt confused and nauseous several times on the way, and prayed that I wouldn't get sick on the bus. I tried to concentrate hard on where I was going and the stop where I needed to get off. Sitting was impossible, so I stood, holding onto a pole for dear life, afraid that

I was going to faint, and nodded "no thanks" when I was offered a seat. Trying to manage a small smile of thanks was painful, and tears welled up in my eyes.

I was outside of myself, looking in. Trying to help this girl get to the dentist, to get help. But I felt . . . fragmented and chaotic . . . separate from her, yet protective. And I was frightened beyond belief that I would see the man somewhere along the way, although I was going in a different direction from his house.

I was at my dentist's office nearly four hours, and when he asked what had happened, my shame made me lie to him and tell him it was a car accident. I don't think he believed me, and there was a part of me that wanted to tell him, but I didn't know how. It was the beginning of many years of shame and silence for me.

He stitched my lower teeth first, then wired my jaw. I knew I was safe in his office, and I never wanted to leave. The combination of feeling ill from all I'd been through, and the anesthesia and medication for pain he gave me, brought a dazed feeling . . . as if none of this was happening and that I was in a dream. The trip home on the bus seemed as if it took forever, though it was only a short distance. Finally arriving home, I lay on my bed, too tired to even take my clothes off except for unzipping my jeans. Friday night was just beginning outside my apartment; the area in which I lived stayed alive until well into the morning. It was even more welcome to me on this night. I needed to hear people around me . . . voices . . . music . . . life . . .

I was exhausted at the end of my appointment with Gary. My chest hurt, my head hurt, even my muscles ached. I hadn't realized how much I'd kept inside. Up until that point in the therapy, I couldn't refer to the rape as a rape; it was an assault, but telling Gary what had happened . . . I could finally say it. He'd helped me to go back into that house and come out again.

I realized that I had been stuck there, in that house for seventeen years.

Chapter 7

September, 1995

My first class with Dr. Preston was on a Wednesday. I looked forward to the subject he was teaching, Family Psychopathology, and to meeting the first male professor we'd had in the program thus far. I'd grown close to each of my female professors and appreciated each of their different therapeutic styles. They shared commonalties such as being nurturing and gentle, and I learned a great deal from each one. I was curious to see how a male would present therapy in an academic setting. I'd been in therapy with Gary nine months and wanted something with which to compare that relationship.

The class was restless prior to his getting there. When he walked into the room, I felt as if a wall had slammed into my head. He was about 6'2" and of average weight for his height. His hair, slightly more reddish-blond, was the same length and style as the man who had raped me. The manner in which his eyebrows framed his eyes, the curve of his jaw bone, his profile . . . all of it reminded me of the other man. He was dressed very professionally in a dark suit, white shirt, and a tie.

Once over the shock of his appearance, I tried to concentrate on his words. I couldn't look at him, though, and kept my nose buried in my book, making copious notes as he talked. The anxiety was overwhelming. Not being able to leave the class made me feel imprisoned in the moment. I recognized this as a trigger to the memory of the man who raped me, and I knew I had no choice but to overcome the feelings ... at least for the next six hours.

I employed all the tools I'd gathered with Gary during therapy for an emergency like this. First I tried the calming breathing exercises, trying to remember Gary's instructions: *Okay, breathing from my abdomen, inhale to the count of five. I can do this. One ... two ... three ... Not so loud. You're still in class. One ... two ... three ... four ... Start over. One ... two ... three ... four ... five. Nothing.*

My heart was still wildly racing, pounding in my ears. I recited Gary's instructions in my head: *Five deep breaths from the abdomen. Just keep doing it. One ... two ... three ... four ... five. One ... two ... three ... four ... five. Wait. There were two normal breaths in between each five count, right? Hadn't Gary told me that? And then the thing he told me to say with those normal breaths ... what was it? Calm? Let go? No. It was "relax."*

I was engaged in this fight for my sanity while the rest of the class went on around me. Terrified that he'd ask us to introduce ourselves, I wrote down on a paper that which most of the professors had asked us to tell them: name (?), what had led me to begin this graduate program (temporary insanity?), what I planned to do with my degree (I'm not sure what I'm planning to do with the next five minutes!). As time wore on, it became obvious that he wasn't going to ask any of those questions, not even our names. *How odd,* I thought, but trying to figure out why he didn't even want to know who we were made me forget his resemblance to the rapist, if only momentarily.

I was still in the middle of this reaction, though, and while my breathing returned somewhat to normal, I knew I had to grab hold of myself as quickly as possible in order to be able to concentrate. I needed to acknowledge the feelings and work them through; there was no other way. I went through my "feelings" list: *Fear? Did I feel unsafe here in the classroom?* No. While he reminded me of the rapist, he wasn't. My logical mind knew I really had nothing to fear from him. His physical appearance reminded me of someone who'd done horrible things to me, but the two men were separate beings. One had nothing to do with the other.

I went back to the list: *Anxiety?* Well, yeah, that fit. The suddenness of seeing someone so similar in appearance had caught me off guard. This was a place that had been, until that moment, safe. Now I perceived it as threatening. My memories of the rapist had invaded yet another place in my life. *Anger?* Yes.

Why was I having such difficulty getting over this? I looked at the clock over my shoulder. I still had four hours to go.

Thinking I had at least a week until I saw Dr. Preston again, I resolved that I'd do more work on getting these feelings under control. This class was crucial, and if this was in my way, I wouldn't benefit from it at all. His words brought me around as he appeared in front of me, placing a syllabus on the desk. The following Saturday was highlighted.

"Sorry, guys, but we're going to be putting in a couple of Saturdays ... time is tight." My heart sank. I wasn't going to see Gary until well after then. I didn't look forward to an entire Saturday with this man just yet.

I slipped into my car that evening after class and put my head on the steering wheel. It felt good to be out of the classroom, away from Dr. Preston and on the way home to my husband. There was a part of me that wanted to call him, tell him I was on my way and to be ready for me to pick him up. And then drive. Anywhere. Anywhere away from here.

I thought about the situation the following Thursday and Friday, and thought about my best course of action. I counted the number of classes I had with Dr. Preston and counted the number of hours. How could I concentrate on the material, admittedly a difficult subject? My instinct was to speak with Dr. Preston and ask his help. As a psychologist, I was confident that he would understand what I was going through; but this wasn't his problem, and this wasn't therapy. Should I be sharing this with him?

When I saw Dr. Preston Saturday morning, he was dressed casually in jeans, a polo shirt and, to my shock, the same type of leather shoes that the rapist had worn that day. I nearly lost my resolve to ask if I could speak with him later, but steeled myself and made arrangements to see him at the first break.

"I have a problem that I need your help with," I started. When I'm nervous, I start talking a mile a minute. I had rehearsed my talk with him for the entire two hours since we started. We'd gone into a small conference room for our discussion.

"What can I help you with?" he asked. His smile was sincere and infectious, and I momentarily regretted having asked to see him. But he leaned back in the chair and stretched his long legs in front of him, his manner making me feel as if I could take my time and collect my thoughts, that I had his full attention. I jumped in with both feet.

"I was raped in a man's house for fourteen hours..." I couldn't believe what I'd just said to this stranger. "...and you look just like him...and I'm having a lot of trouble with this." Tears welled up in the corners of my eyes and spilled onto my cheeks. I was still explaining this hell seventeen years later. I felt as if my heart had been tightly trussed with string and someone had suddenly cut it. My chest actually hurt. "...and," I went on, not letting him get a word in "...you have shoes on just like he did." My tone was accusatory, but I didn't mean for it to be. We both looked down at his shoes.

He leaned forward and placed his elbows on his knees, bringing his hands together. "I told my wife these shoes were too old. I got them in the '70's." His eyes met mine. They were warm and compassionate and relayed the fact that he was respectful of the chance I'd taken, easing my embarrassment. "Teresa...I'm sorry that you've had to go through this, but I think you did the right thing in telling me. It'll explain any time you might just be zoning out in class. I'll expect good work from you because I know you can do it, but I am sorry for what you've been through."

I took a breath. I hadn't realized I'd been holding it so long. My progress seemed so slow sometimes, so minuscule. But at moments like this, moments I couldn't have hoped for because I'd never known that intimacy in such situations took place, I was heartened that my feeling would change.

And he never wore those shoes to class again, which was kind of him.

At first, I couldn't wait to tell Gary what I'd done. I was so pleased that I'd recognized what was happening and had taken action, and I thought he'd be proud of my progress. After some thought, though, I wondered if that was a good idea. His approval of me lately had become very important to me. I felt as if I was becoming *too* dependent on him, *too* anxious to have him think highly of me. Had I done this for myself, or for him? Why wasn't it simply enough to have done it for myself?

Chapter

November, 1995

"Please help me get out of that house. Please."

Phil's sweater hung to my knees; it was huge on me. I felt small and child-like in it and wanted to just crawl up on Gary's couch and cry. The weather was stormy and mirrored my mood. I told Gary that I was sure I was going to die a violent death at the hands of someone. On or off. Black or white. All or nothing. I'm bad. Always have been.

"What you went through was brutal, Teresa."

I was taken aback by Gary's words, and a feeling of shame came over me. *No, I thought. Other people have been through worse. Don't talk about it anymore. It's over. It's out.* And I didn't like the word *brutal*, probably because it was the truth.

The feeling of freedom I'd felt after telling Gary about the rape was fading, and the old feeling of restlessness was returning. I felt resistance again. *I should be better. This should be over.* But it wasn't. There was a scene during the rape that I was obsessing over, and I didn't know why.

My guilt, he told me, was irrational. The mood swings, the terror, the inability to relate to others, the flashbacks, he reminded me, wouldn't necessarily go away right away; in fact, they might not be alleviated for quite a while. We were still taking lids off what I'd repressed. *Still . . . after eleven months?* I remember thinking. *How long is this going to go on? I've told you everything.*

Earlier in my therapy, I anticipated moments of awareness, but it was clear to me as I sat there that it's not one moment, but rather a collection of moments that lead to insight. Periods of clarity and truth, of lightness and confidence in myself and the actions I'd taken, were fleeting and few in the beginning, but slowly were becoming more frequent and lasting.

"The surgery went well, I think." I changed the subject. It was my first appointment at Gary's private office; finally I'd be seeing him every week, and that was on my mind. "I think it did, anyway." I rubbed my jaw as I spoke. I was still embarrassed by his attention to the brutality of the rape.

The surgery to repair my jaw, still a problem for me, had gone well, but I was in a great deal of pain still and didn't really know what to talk about. I had a strange feeling of wanting to be left alone, yet needed to be there with him.

And I suppose I felt as if I was in a transitional period of some sort. A vague feeling of being *between*. Of not really knowing which direction I was going and whether the things I was feeling, thoughts I was having, were in fact going to change me for the better.

"Initially, I thought I'd only be in Michigan for four or five days . . . maybe a week. I had to get home and get my life straightened out. I was fortunate to have Lisa, a friend since sixth grade, to stay with . . . " I sighed. I'd changed the subject completely, but I was as mystified as to why, as Gary seemed to be.

Silence. Respectful silence that I ached to fill. And why was I talking about this? It had nothing . . . well, *little* to do with the rape, except for timing. *Leave it alone. Don't muddy the water.*

" . . . and," I went on, "I couldn't . . . still can't separate my dad's death from the rape. It was too close in time. The rape started on a Thursday at 4:30 in the afternoon, and I finally made it home at about 6:30 the following morning. About fourteen hours. My dad was killed the following day, and I was on the train to Michigan the next day. That was . . . Sunday. He died on June 19th, two days after the rape began."

I didn't look at Gary with the last sentence. I couldn't. I didn't want him to see any further inside me than I'd already let him. I didn't want him to see how much I needed him right then. More silence. Respectful still, but like a huge, empty canyon that needed to be filled. I stared at the blinds covering the window and pressed my body deeper into the couch. I wanted to lay my head on the armrest, bring my feet up on the couch and cry.

My feelings lately of shame and guilt and disgust with myself were unrelenting. I felt numb and unable to work. I just didn't care. I counted the days until an appointment with Gary, then said nothing or stared into space, afraid to open up old wounds. I felt as if I was in a struggle with both him and Phil, a struggle to make them believe I was as bad as I felt I was, but neither of them would. They gave me compassion, but it was like a drug. While it felt good when I got it, it was more awful than before when it faded. And Gary's compassion? Sometimes it felt as if I were paying for it, like sex. The goal, I knew, was to develop compassion for myself, for the girl on the mattress, but I was dry. I had none. None for myself, anyway.

Anger. Hidden and secret. I kept it tucked away, deep down inside. I was very practiced at hiding my rage. The power of it scared me. Really scared me. *What might I do if it "got out?" Would I be out of control?* I'd painted a huge red "R" for rape on my forehead, and since talking to Gary about what had happened, I felt as if it had burned into my skin.

Lately I'd been hearing the man's voice in my head when it was quiet, his face close to mine, his mouth against my ear so close that I could smell him. He talked to me in a low, guttural voice, telling me the things he was going to do to me. Knowing it was coming, anticipating the pain he was going to put me through, was pure agony . . . to know the torture that was coming. Now, being here in Gary's office, the man's voice rang in my ears again. All I wanted was to be let out of this prison I kept myself in.

I looked into Gary's eyes. They were soft and kind and understanding of my pain. Tears rolled down my cheeks as I tried to find words that would make sense, that would make a difference if I said them, but my sentences sounded incoherent. My words mixed with the man's words in my mind, and my eyes burned from the tears.

In my purse, I had the journal from the box I'd had the courage to open yesterday. The box marked *Death*.

I wondered for a moment if I should tell Gary about the boxes, about going over memories that probably had a lot to do with what I was going through. I wondered if I should tell him of sitting on the edge of the bed looking at the boxes with the colors that reminded me of Christmas, and looking inside: my dad's wallet with a TWA credit card and an Experimental Aircraft Association membership card, his driver's license and pilot's license. And a picture of me, at twelve. I turned it over. On the back, I'd written *To Daddy. A loving, wonderful, and nice man. Love Teresa.* I wondered if I should tell him all that.

I've always felt that the relationship between a girl and her father colors each of her subsequent relationships with men. At that moment, I wanted Gary to be my father. I wanted him to tell me that I mattered. That I mattered to him.

I wanted to tell him about the photograph of my dad I found in the box. When I found it, I ran my fingers across it. I wanted to feel him one more time. He stood underneath a palm dressed in a tan uniform that fit smoothly over his chest and stomach. His arms, visible from under the short sleeves, were even more muscular in real life. I felt a feverish energy when he wrapped them around me. It had been so long that the memory was nearly faded, but the desire remained. The tension in his forearms made me want him to hold me even closer. They sheltered me from harm. Had that been my desire, or my reality? I wasn't sure.

The fading black and white photograph didn't capture the bronze hue of his skin, almost light ebony against his soft, azure eyes. It did show his eyelashes though, long and black and curling toward the sky. When he laughed, his eyes danced and drew me into him. His smile was infectious, and I savored it when it was directed at me. My relationship with my dad always seemed more of a fantasy than a wish. We moved closer, became too close, then moved away from each other. Elusive.

Deeper inside the box were items from his funeral. The flag that had been draped over his casket. The funeral program and the guest book were further down inside the box.

"I saw a young girl with her father at Mervyn's the other day," I said to Gary, out of the blue. In my mind somewhere, it was connected to the discussion we were having about my dad, I suppose.

"And . . . " Gary was still listening. Sometimes I went away for what seemed like a long time, and I was surprised he was still sitting there listening. But he was, and he remembered.

"She was helping him pick out clothes, matching this color with that . . . these pants with that shirt . . . and asked him to come out of the dressing room to show her how they looked on him. She waited for him to return and called out several times to ask how he was doing. He came out dressed in his old clothes, and her face dropped. She asked him why he didn't come out to show her, and he said they looked just fine, so what was the point in showing her that?" I took a breath. Tears were welling up in my eyes, thinking of how his comeback stung her. The pain was so evident on her face.

"So how does this relate to what you were telling me about your dad?" Gary asked. He was practiced at weaving my memories together, helping me realize how they all related. I was the one falling down on the job, though. I just didn't get it many times.

"I don't know. I just . . . I wonder why fathers don't realize what they do to their daughters. People talk about abuse, but they don't talk about indifference."

I glanced at the clock on the table beside me. Although we had a couple of minutes left, I wanted to leave; in fact, I resisted the urge to jump out of my seat.

"I wish my dad could have met my husband, learned how I turned out. I wish he could've seen how much Phil loves me . . . I miss him so badly."

I slipped into the driver's seat after leaving the appointment. It was still cold and rainy, and I felt more lonely than ever. I'd forgotten that I'd brought the journal from the box marked *Death* to show to Gary, but had chickened out. I knew Phil wasn't available for lunch, and it was early. I drove to Valley Fair and parked the car. I didn't want to go home, so I grabbed a cup of coffee and sat with the journal . . .

June 19, 1976

The phone jolted me awake this morning. Yesterday doesn't exist. This has been hell. The words came across the phone like a dream. Heard only bits and pieces. "Dad . . . air show . . . killed . . . plane accident . . . huge crowd . . . no one else hurt . . . "

What? What? I wanted to ask the nurse questions, but my face was cracked and bloody from sleeping. I hadn't even talked to anyone yet. I wasn't used to breathing yet.

She thought I was in shock from what she told me, and handed the phone to a friend of Daddy's. I think she said she would take care of all the necessary plans and would have the funeral held as soon as I got to town. The phone went dead. I think. I don't remember. I don't remember anything.

I know he's in Niles this weekend, but this has to be some sick joke. I'll wake up tomorrow and none of this will have happened. I'll go to Michigan and straighten all this out. I don't want to go. I don't know what to do.

I sat there in bed this morning for a long time trying to figure out what to do. What on earth was happening to my life? All I want to do is sleep, but all I see when I close my eyes is yesterday. I remember leaving a message for Rick last night with his service, telling him that someone in my family died. Oh God, what have I done? I was talking about me . . .

June 23, 1976

The funeral today was excruciating. A bundle of desire and cravings and needs and longings. That's what I remember about Daddy. I had his photograph with me when I got to the funeral home, and all I could do was hold on tighter when I first saw his casket. The trip from Michigan was such a long one, difficult and lonely. Two and a half days. I still feel as if I'm jumping out of my skin with all that has happened.

I asked the funeral director to let me see him, but because of his injuries, they said they had to insist upon a closed casket. The wondering of what he looks like, looked like, seems worse than just seeing him and getting it over with. I want to see what his body looks like. What his arms look like. To imagine him holding me. I want to know for sure that it's him, that he's really dead. I can't believe I'm being forced to do this. The funeral director said I seemed too fragile. If only they knew. In any case, they wouldn't bend the rules for me, saying it was in my own best interests.

A lot of people showed up for Daddy's funeral. He'd have been very happy to have seen them all, if only to know that people he's known throughout his life, pilots he's flown with, cared so much. But their faces are a blur. Even if what happened hadn't happened, this would have been a horrid experience. As it was, I was just trying to get through it so I could lie down. I felt so dizzy and nauseous through most of it.

Aunt Helen and Aunt Margaret came over to me just after I got to the funeral home and gave me a beautiful gold and silver locket with Daddy's name and birth date. They were both more heavy and stocky than I remembered, and I could tell they were both coloring their hair now. They were more like Grandma than I'd ever noticed. I could just picture a kerchief around their hair, throwing chicken seed on the ground, though I've never seen them actually do that.

Aunt Helen pulled me aside and asked how I came to look "like this." I told her it was a car accident. She said she knew better and that I knew what I had to do. Her words keep coming back to me.

Does she know? Does everyone know? How could she know what happened? What do I need to do? I convinced myself after that bout of paranoia on the train that nobody would know what happened to me, but now I wonder. It doesn't matter, in any case. I probably won't see her again; she's gone home already, and I won't get up north before I leave. But is it obvious that I was raped? Do I really have a huge red "R" for rape on my forehead? I don't know where to turn, my head is spinning so. I want to be in the darkness with Daddy.

They brought a picture for the top of his casket: him in his Navy uniform. He was eighteen and had just gotten his uniform for this first "official" picture. He looked so handsome. The picture was colorized, but his face, his smile, was full of youth and promise and a life yet to be lived. Too many people to count came up and told me that I looked like I was his sister. He was younger than me when the picture was taken.

I'm still angry at Mom for not coming. She was still so angry at him from the divorce. But she should be here with me right now. It gives her no right to do this to me. I can't do this alone.

I have no idea what I'm doing. I sat there listening to the priest. I couldn't believe what he was saying. He spoke about Daddy as if he'd known him. I sat there with my hands folded, bandaged and throbbing. Everyone insisted on holding my hands as they kissed my swollen cheeks.

My face is a kaleidoscope of purple. All shades from light to dark. Ribbons of bruises making their way across my face, down my arms and legs, all over me. Most of the damage is inside, though, where other people can't see it. I can't seem to stop looking at the colors on my skin. Some have a deep purple hue, some are more pastel.

Everyone had questions for me today. How? What happened? And from people who hadn't seen the plane . . . had I been in the accident with my father? A car accident, I explain through the wires in my jaw. Who gives a shit. The truth is so distressing, I'm not sure I'll ever be able to tell anyone what happened. The truth is confusing me. I need explanation. I have no space inside me that's private anymore.

I don't know who I am. I'm thinking thoughts I don't understand. I'm confused and feel like sleeping, yet can't close my eyes. Can't settle down. I want to escape from everything around me. I feel as if I'm being pressed forward by a crowd of people who are moving me around the room. My feet are off the floor, and I'm being carried between everyone's shoulders. I'm being moved around the room. I'm being moved around my life. My actions for the last several days have been laid out for me . . . go to the dentist . . . go home . . . answer the phone . . . get on the train . . . go to the funeral . . . as if someone has planned a sadistic itinerary for me that I had no say in planning. No say in where I'd end up. No choices. I have no idea what's happened to my life in only a few short days.

I started crying at the funeral for everything that had happened. The rape, the pain, Daddy. I need someone to hold me. I wish he was here now so I could talk to him. I *loved his sense of humor. Am I ever going to laugh again? I never told him how much he meant to me. I never told him how much I loved his sense of humor. As soon as one of us got too close to the other, we'd make a joke to take the pressure off. I needed him to show me how to be a woman . . . a wife. Now he's gone. I wonder if I could have told him about what happened. No. I don't think so. If he disapproved of me, if he abandoned me, I'd have no one. I'd be all alone. I am all alone.*

June 28, 1976

I had to go alone to Daddy's house today. I couldn't get anyone to go with me, but I had to go. I had to get started cleaning it out. Everyone thinks it'll be depressing, and now everything is sort of settling down anyway. Everyone's going back home. It's strange to see all the friends I grew up with. To realize we're all adults now. I don't feel like it at all. I feel like a scared little girl.

This house. So many memories. So many tears. So many years ago, but it feels like yesterday. And it's the same as it was when we left, only it looks smaller than when I was a child, of course. Up the same cobblestone road, across the street from the same scary house, next door to Mr. Kreiger's. The same living room and fireplace looking out over the same forest of lush trees. Only things are different now.

There were thousands of little bugs, all lying dead on the steps. It was strange. The wide, green steps leading up to the house needed painting, and the house did too. The white and green awning he'd put up years ago was gone. He'd been so proud of that awning. I wondered what he did with it.

As a kid, I liked looking out of the front windows at the trees across the street. They were most beautiful in the winter. The spindly, dark branches reaching toward the sky but bending, laden with heavy snow. And at night when the old-fashioned street lamp shown on the soft, new snow, the future felt hopeful.

I pushed against the screen door. It still wasn't fixed, but that didn't surprise me. Daddy was always busy with something bigger. I was surprised by the furniture in the living room, though. He'd decorated it in a sort of country style. I never knew he liked that. Mom's such a . . . minimalist type person. The less around, the better. The less said, the better. I remember one year on her birthday, he wanted to buy her a new living room set so we went to Sears together to pick one out. The first one we looked at was sort of country style, like what he had in his house now. It was pretty and I liked it, but I thought Mom would hate it. I told him so, but now I'm so sorry I said anything. He must have thought I was criticizing his taste. I want to tell him I'm sorry, but I can't. This is the first time in my life that I've wanted to talk to someone but can't. I'll never be able to call him or write to him. He's gone, and I feel incredibly alone.

I looked up and noticed a 3x5 card taped on the inside of the front door. (1) Feed Snowball (2) Turn off the lights (3) Check on Mr. Kreiger. On and on. A whole checklist of tasks he'd made before leaving. Just like me: a master list-maker. He probably looked at this card the morning he was killed. He probably glanced at it and checked off each item in his mind, and walked out the door thinking he would be back, but he never made it. How can any of us know where life's journey will take us?

June 30, 1976

I know my isolation following their divorce was self-imposed. I didn't want to be around anyone. Every week after getting my paycheck, I'd go to the animal shelter and buy another small, pitiful package of fur and take it home, determined to nourish it back to health, to love it like no one else had, to add the new puppy to my menagerie or in some cases to find another loving home for them. I'd bathe them first, softly lathering their fur, then rinsing them. As they shook the water off wildly . . . even the smallest of puppies . . . I and the others in the menagerie would watch as the new kid on the block ran playfully through the house . . . I wanted them all to be loved, and taken care of, and safe. I'd take all of them into the back yard and play until they were tired, and then we'd all troop back in the house for dinner. Later, when getting ready for bed, all the puppies would end up on my bed with me. Very Dr. Doolittle. And it worked beautifully . . . until Dana.

She was the smallest puppy I'd ever seen. Abandoned by the side of the road at six weeks, she was kept alive by the staff at the animal shelter. . . barely. She was sweet, the color of taffy with huge, dark brown pools of chocolate for eyes. And she still had puppy breath.

"You don't want her . . . she's not very healthy . . . she may not make it." The man's voice came from behind me, but his warning had come too late. She was mine. I'd already decided I could give her what she needed. I took her immediately to the vet, who by this time was getting to know me quite well. He confirmed what the man at the shelter had told me, but felt that with medication and lots of attention, she might have a chance.

I listened intently as he gave me instructions. I asked if I could give her a bath when I got her home. He said there would be no problem. With the other puppies and Snowball, the queen, watching, she ran through the house as the others had, delighting in the water flying off her back.

Later, though, she grew tired quickly. When Snowball and I took the rest of the puppies into the back yard, Dana wanted only to curl up onto my lap. She seemed to crave my petting, my caresses, because when I stopped, she would gently nudge my hand with her nose and I would begin again.

We stayed in the back yard long into the evening, until it grew cold. One by one, the puppies grew tired as well and joined Snowball, Dana, and myself, until they surrounded us on the grass. Unwilling to disturb her rest, I allowed her to just enjoy the love she was getting for the first time in her short life.

The struggle to regain her health was hard for her because her medical problem, a heartworm, is a deadly serious problem to dogs, particularly puppies. There were times when I could see that it was getting the best of her. It had been five weeks since I brought her home, and my love for her just grew deeper every day.

Her vet appointment that morning was going to be difficult to get to . . . a snowstorm had nearly all the roads blocked . . . but I had to get her there. She'd taken a turn for the worse; the medication was not strong enough to combat the heartworm. "You've done all you can, Teresa . . . leave her here with me," the vet said, trying to console me . . . to stem the tears he saw in my eyes.

No. No, if she dies . . . when she dies . . . it's going to be in my home. It's going to be in my arms with Snowball and the other puppies she's played with. I didn't want her to be alone with a stranger holding her. I paid for the visit, and for another round of medicine for her. It could be two to three weeks before she died, and the medication might ease her pain a bit.

The weather had turned even colder than it had been when I first arrived at the vet's office. She was shivering already, so I wrapped her in her baby blanket and put her on the seat next to me, against my leg. I turned on the heater and aimed the vents down to warm her, and we started home. The streets were icy, and the car slipped every which way. I was used to driving in ice . . . sleet . . . snow . . . but this was so treacherous it was beginning to frighten me. I was scared to death that we'd have an accident on the way home.

Turning up Sloan Lane, God, I must've been at least three miles away still, I felt the back end of the car slide to the right. I had no steering. No power. I reached down and held tight to Dana and frantically tried to keep the car on the road. Straightening out, I brought it to a stop along the side and put my head on the steering wheel. The engine had stalled.

I looked down at Dana. Her beautifully expressive brown eyes were looking up at me, and her tail gave a tiny wag visible under the little baby blanket. She was getting tired, and I had to get her home . . . I had to give her her medication and dinner.

I tried starting the car. Nothing. Again. Nothing. This time I pumped the gas furiously. Still nothing. Was I flooding it, or was it the damn battery again? Since the *divorce, money was scarce, and a new battery cost money. We had the number of the tow truck driver memorized, he came out to jump-start us so often. The choice between money for Dana's medicine and a new battery was easy. But now I was afraid it was dead for good.*

Sloan Lane wasn't traveled very often, particularly in the winter because of the dangerous curves; but it was the shortest distance between two points for me, which is why I took it that day. With the car stuck, I had no other choice but to walk and hope that someone would give me a ride home. I couldn't leave Dana there by herself, even though it was still warm in the car. It would probably take me two hours to walk home, and it would get terribly cold in the car by the time I got back with help.

I wrapped Dana in her baby blanket, talking to her the whole time. I had on a thick, large winter parka, and I opened it, then opened my sweater and my shirt. I gathered her up in my arms and put her against my chest, thinking that might give her the most warmth. I held her around her bottom and buttoned my shirt, then my sweater, and finally zipped my parka, leaving room for her head.

We started out. I whispered in her ear that we'd be home soon and that I'd take care of her. We walked for what seemed like hours but was only about a half hour or so. The wind was biting; it felt as if shards of glass were landing against my face, and it was snowing heavier than it had been. The side of the road dropped off sharply on both sides, so I walked in the road most of the time. Slipping and sliding, I put my thumb out when the only two cars passed me. No one stopped. Bastards . . . I remember muttering under my breath. I had a puppy that I needed to get home. I kept singing softly so that she wouldn't be scared.

I looked down at Dana, but she wasn't looking back at me like she had been. Placing my hand on the top of her head, I started petting her fur. More briskly now. Nothing. Don't do this to me, Dana. Don't do this. I brought her chin up and looked in her eyes . . . they were drooping and looked so tired.

I stopped walking and held her to my chest. Tears welled up in my eyes, and I bit hard into my lip, trying to stop crying. All at once a sigh emitted from her tiny body. An immense sigh for how small she was, and a shudder that shook her tiny body. I took her back out from inside my parka and held her toward me. Her eyes were closed, and her head flopped ever so softly to the left. Sobbing, I cried for her to come back, but heard only my lonely wails mixed with the wind. She had left me.

July 7, 1976

Today was the hardest time being in Daddy's house. I sat looking at the planks of the hardwood floor he'd refinished. The sun shown on them so beautifully. Where there used to be an ugly, awful carpet, pools of butterscotch swirls invited you to walk upon them. To stay. To enjoy. But I can't. I hate this house and I hate the way it makes me feel and I hate that it's empty and I hate that Daddy's gone.

I was sixteen when I got rid of that ugly carpet. And it was their fault. The divorce was difficult, and I was angry. I never felt like I could show it, though. I remember looking at that ugly, awful carpet, and suddenly I just had to get rid of it. I was tired. Tired of trying to hold our little family together. Tired of being the only one who cared. And real tired of that carpet. I had rage with no release valve. The time, the energy I invested in holding us all together was wasted. My effort was worse than wasted because it showed me that I was the only one who cared.

The carpet was heavy. Like my life. It weighed me down in a way I couldn't define. So one day while Mom was at work, I got rid of it. It was huge, and I was exhausted rolling it up, but with every turn of the carpet, I rolled up parts of my life. They had yanked the carpet from under me and then, there I was, tugging the carpet up at the baseboards, snapping tacks along the edges. I watched as they twirled up toward the ceiling, somersaulted, caught the light like diamonds, and fell back to Earth like little stars.

I need a fucking carpet to rip up right now. My mind is consumed with the rape and Daddy's death. I can't close my eyes because all I see is one or the other. The man's face. My dead father. I ache for someone to talk to. I'm frightened of being alone and want to be with someone all the time, yet want to be alone. When I'm alone, though, I can't seem to get past one or two thoughts without crying, so it's easier just staying busy. Hanging around with someone all the time. It just makes me feel numb, though, and I'm not sure that's in my best interest in the long run. What if this all explodes out of me one day? What will I do to myself?

I've lost so much.

July 17, 1976

Mr. Zabert called today and wanted to see me right away. I nearly cried when he gave me the news. Daddy left no will, so I'll have to stay and testify that I'm his only heir in order to tie everything up. It may take months, he said. I don't want to stay here with Lisa, but I have nowhere else to go, and no money. I feel guilty. She's been very kind to

me, but things are becoming hard for us. Just the fact that I know I can't go home is
making me tense and cranky at her, and I'm sorry for that. All I see is time stretching out
in front of me, and I'm raw. All I can think about is the rape and Daddy and . . . I just
feel so sad all the time. The only escape I can get is going to the movies.

I thought Lisa and I were as close as two friends could be . . . sisters . . . but something
has changed between us. Too many things have taken place in our lives since I left Michigan, I guess, that the other wasn't a part of. We used to love talking about what we were
going to do in the future, and I suppose I feel like she has one now and I don't.

And this apartment. I'm so depressed being here, especially alone. It's spacious, but
there are ominous reminders all over that it's a converted funeral home. Little areas,
nooks and crannies, hold reminders of what was here before. And having just gone through
Daddy's funeral . . . well, I don't like being here. It makes me feel skittish. The only other
place, though, is Daddy's house, but that's worse. I couldn't sleep there; it's all I can do
to just be there alone.

Mr. Zabert said he needed a full inventory of the stuff in the basement, so I went
down there today. I begged Lisa to come with me, but she made excuse after excuse. It
took me forever to get up the nerve. It felt freaky being down there alone; I never did like
it at all. Everything was as I remember it. Rows and rows of manuals on the left side, his
photography equipment on the right, all his darkroom stuff, and the long table at the end.
And on top of the table were his typewriter and my old record player. I remember when he
bought me that, and some records too. I couldn't help it; I just started crying.

I sat down on the steps, remembering the times we spent in the basement. I loved
helping him with his airplanes. No job too small. Whatever he needed, whether it was
cutting fabric or gluing . . . whatever . . . I just wanted to be near him. We didn't talk much,
or if we did it, was just joking around, laughing, never about anything serious. And when
we flew it for the first time . . . I loved seeing the shadow of the plane on the calm, smooth
water beneath us, a shadow plane bringing us safely home. I miss him so much.

I wonder how many people saw him crash. I hope not too many children. The
silence, the deafening silence is what I remember after the crashes I've seen. Deafening.

August 15, 1976

Being in Daddy's house is disconcerting. I grew up here, but the more time I spend
here with his things, the more scared I become. I was sitting in the living room today
going through his papers, and I heard a noise in the basement. I ran to the basement
door but stood there frozen. I couldn't move. Again. I was sick to my stomach with

fright. It was so hard with my jaw wired shut. I was sick for about an hour. I just couldn't move my head.

This panic is paralyzing me. I can't talk to anyone, yet I'm living it. Every single second of every single day. When will these feelings end? It's been over a month. I should be better by now.

I don't feel like I'm able to concentrate on anything anymore. I just feel lost.

I put the journal on the seat next to me. This had all happened a lifetime ago . . . to someone else, it seemed, but it was me. A young, naive, painfully shy, me. I'd stuffed the white envelope into the back of the journal and thought about opening it, but lost my courage. I couldn't look inside. Not now.

Chapter

December, 1995

We followed the gentle turn in the road and saw the bay stretched out in front of us. I was glad to have the diversion of leaving town with Phil for several days. It had been weeks since I last saw Gary, yet I kept going over and over our conversation. Could he see in my soul, or was it simply, as he said, that he knew me now?

It had been some time since I'd ventured into the boxes. I was apprehensive and clearly more comfortable with the complacence of not facing what they had to teach me, than the pain they awoke. *Therapy must be working. At least now I know when I'm in denial,* I thought with a wry smile. As a last-minute thought while packing for the trip, I opened the box marked *Birth* and reached in to grab the journal, not really sure if I'd be up to reading it on the trip. The pain was much too deep in this box to stay very long.

A rattle and several small bibs. A book on birth. The first time I looked at the book — sometime in my fifth or sixth month of pregnancy, I suppose — I remember being transfixed by the pictures of women giving birth. The look of deep concentration and supreme effort on their faces was no less than beautiful to me. I opened it again and wondered if that was what I looked like when I was in labor. While groping inside the box for papers, I came across a stack of pamphlets paper-banded together: *How to Breast Feed Your Baby. The Joys of Motherhood. Eating for Two.*

My back fell against the wall. I remembered picking these up at the clinic, reading them, clutching them in my hands when the woman returned to give me the results of the pregnancy test, but nothing more. I couldn't begin to speculate on why I'd brought them back from Michigan, what purpose they served for me at the time. My head began to ache. The anniversary of her birth was upon me again, the hideous and petrifying gift of the rapist . . . a child.

We finally settled into our room at the lodge in Bodega Bay, about four hours north of San Francisco, at 6:30, becoming more and more relaxed after crossing the Golden Gate Bridge. The room had a cathedral ceiling, a fireplace, and was warm and inviting. Phil started a fire right away. We looked out of the patio window at our view; while it was dark out already, we could make out the stately figures of reed grass blowing ever so softly by the light of the moon. Their gentle sway and the soft licking of the water on the beach further down was soothing. Phil turned me toward him and took my face in his hands to give me a kiss.

After a long, relaxing supper at the restaurant lodge just down a gentle slope from our room, Phil suggested I take a hot bath. I ran the water, the steam forming a soft mist in the room and looked at myself in the mirror. How I'd changed. I was silhouetted against the sea green shower curtain. A woman's body; a child's emotions. I ran my hand over my breasts, over the scars from the candle wax, and was surprised at how much I longed for a baby to hold to my breast, to nurture and love.

I drew the bath much hotter than necessary. I always crossed the line between a pleasantly warm bath and an excruciatingly hot one, as if I wanted to burn the memory of the man off my skin, still. I dipped my toe in first and then my leg, watching it grow a rosy pink, then a blazing red, and forced myself down into the water. Forced myself to accept the heat. What I continued to try to prove to myself, I do not know. That I could accept pain? That I couldn't be broken?

I picked up the journal from the small table alongside the tub.

September 29, 1976

I'm not sure whether I've had my period or not. I haven't stopped bleeding since the rape, and I'm scared. Ever since that day on the train, I haven't stopped bleeding, so I called the clinic today. They told me they wouldn't see me without a pregnancy test. I told them that it was unrelated, I was sure, but . . . they insisted. Lisa told me that she'd be there for me no matter what, and I'm grateful, even though our relationship seems to be going through some kind of "growing pains."

October 10, 1976

Shit. Shit. The rape had finally started to dull ever so slightly around the edges. No reminders to haunt me here. No man. No house. No feelings. And now this. I don't think I can take any more. The girl at the clinic wasn't much younger than me.

"Teresa . . . Teresa . . ." Her words seemed so far away, but it was her hand shaking my shoulder that made me look at the her. " . . . you're pregnant."

A statement with no room for questions. Her eyes searched mine for reaction. Was this expected . . . or not? She wanted me to provide the right follow-up proclamation, but I couldn't provide it. Or wouldn't. I'm not sure which. I was stunned.

My mouth ached and the blood drained from my face. The urge to put my fist through the wall was nearly impossible to ignore, but instead I turned away from the pamphlets I'd been staring at and ran to the car. I slammed the door harder than I'd intended and rocked the car back and forth. I just sat there crying with my head on the steering wheel. When is this hell going to end?

I can't believe this. I can't believe this. I can't believe this. How can I be so unlucky?

Her words have brought the rape right back into sharp focus. He's still raping me. All I see is red. All I feel is blinding fury. I can't take any more of these emotions. I'm trying so hard to make sense of everything, but all I feel is confusion and chaos.

So here I am, wondering how the hell I got here. The dunes. I'm not sure how the hell I got here. Always my place of comfort. The water is so blue. Azure. It's the color of Daddy's eyes before me as far as I can see. What would happen if I just started walking. Down the dunes, across the road, down the beach, into the water . . . and into the water . . . and in and in and further in. It's difficult to breathe. I'm panting. Keep writing, Teresa. Keep writing . . . it will get better. I can't get any air into my lungs.

I've been bleeding since the rape. Maybe they're wrong; maybe I should have told them what happened. Maybe he hurt me and it gave a false reading on the test. I just keep looking down at my stomach. I want to pull out whatever he's put inside me. I can't believe this. There must be some mistake. Four hours have gone by since I left the clinic, and I can't move. All I can do is sit here and write and cry . . . cry and write. I'm losing time again. *Episodes of just being somewhere where I don't remember how I got there. I'm not even making sense any more. But I'm having more of these, and I have to get control of myself. I feel numb and overwhelmed and alone. And so very sad. Each time it happens, I promise I'll talk to someone about it. But what if I'm going nuts and they commit me? What would I do then? I'm so scared.*

I wish Snowball was here with me. My baby. I miss the time we'd sit up here and watch the sun slide into the horizon, lying back and letting the soft breezes play against us, puffing the sweet smell of mint julep that lined the road. Her fur felt so heavy and silken between my fingers. So rich. Will I ever have such a best friend again? Will I ever have someone who accepts me like she did?

October 30, 1976

My days are filled with phone calls to clinics, but the answer is always the same. Too far along. Nothing can be done now, "dear." A condescending "dear" always follows their statement, intending to be an admonition. It just makes me more angry. Today the clinics I called were all the way in Chicago. I just don't know what to do. Still, the answer is always the same. I heard myself begging . . . I'll take my chances. The alternative . . . I can't think of it . . . it's too horrendous.

I don't want to deliver this child. I'm sure it's a little girl. I can't imagine looking in her face and seeing the man who raped me. How can I be sure she'll be normal? That she'll be all right physically and mentally? I'm trying so hard to do the right thing. She's the only person more innocent than me in this nightmare.

Lisa and I were lying in bed yesterday evening when she reached for my hand. "What does it feel like?" she asked. "What does it really feel like . . . being pregnant?"

I took her hand and put it on my thigh on top of my nightgown. Her hand pushed the material into my skin. "Feel," I said, moving her hand to my stomach. I hadn't realized how large the baby had grown. It's almost November, and I'm nearly five months pregnant. I haven't had the courage to touch myself since the rape, let alone look in a mirror. I feel no connection to my body. No connection to my soul. I can't really tell any more what I feel. Am I hot? Cold? Am I hungry? Full? I don't know any more. I've always been in awe of birth, but all I could do at that moment was cry from deep down inside, all the pain of the last four and a half months erupting out of me.

We talked long into the night like old times. It feels, I whispered to her, mysterious and strange. I've gained a certain acceptance, I suppose, that I'm going to have the baby and put her up for adoption. My feelings are a patchwork of regret and wonder

and anger and amazement . . . of fascination at how my body is changing, but resent-
ment at how my body is changing. Pain, terrible pain all the way down into my heart.
The conflict between what I want to do and . . . what I have to do. Shit.

She never asked who the father was, and I was careful not to tell her I'd been raped,
though I'm tired of holding this secret inside. I'm not sure why I don't feel like I can tell
her. I just can't. I don't want to hurt her. There's a part of me, though, that wants her to
ask me. I feel as if we're trying to ignore this big thing in the room.

Lisa raised my nightgown and laid her hand on my bare stomach. It felt so good.
Her hand was so warm and soft, and her fingers moved ever so slightly across me. I felt
the baby pulling my skin tight. She has grown so large. I just kept crying as Lisa traced
these small circles onto my stomach. I want someone to touch me with tenderness. I want
her to do it again.

She buried her face deep inside my hair, right next to my ear. Her breathing was
steady but raspy, and it matched the pressure she exerted against my stomach. The sensa-
tion of having a child inside me, closer than any other being, was one that I had ached for
all my life. This feeling, though, the one I need so bad, is mixed with feeling dirty and
hideous and ruined. What am I carrying inside me? Who was the man who raped me?
He's damaged me, emotionally, beyond repair.

She brought my hand up and placed it on my stomach ever so gently, and then she
moved my hand around in circular motions like she had. I felt parts of the baby inside
me. Astounding! I hadn't wanted to feel this, but now that I have, I'm grateful for the
sensation. I moved my hands to my breasts. They'd grown so big. My nipples are so
tender, but hard at the same time. I touched myself and the baby and felt the warmth
returning to me for the first time since the rape. Lisa put her hands on my thighs and
started massaging me ever so softly until I must have fallen asleep.

This is so unfair. The empathy, the bond that I feel for the baby is complete. This is
going to be terribly difficult for me, no matter the outcome. My heart aches so bad.

November 1, 1976

I stood at the top of the stairs late this afternoon. Silent. Unmoving. One small
gesture, one small step and we would be gone. I stood there without sound or movement,
gathering my courage. I was the only one home. If I was to do this, it had to be at that
moment. The only sound was a slight rustling of leaves from a soft November wind. The
image of the leaves . . . of soft, muted tones of orange and brown and gold, feather light,
catching the wind and falling to the deep green earth, brought tears to my eyes. Warm

tears that streaked my face and wouldn't stop. Suddenly clouding everything in front of me was a fist. It slammed first against my front teeth, then against my jaw. Disconnected from a body, it was gone as fast as it had appeared, but it left me reeling.

My hand groped in front of me, finding only air. My heart beat wildly. The wall on the opposite side, framing the huge mahogany staircase, blurred, then spun wildly out of control. My hand clamped down hard, finding the huge wood ball at the top of the banister. Still holding on, I dropped to the top step, then fell onto my back.

I want to die. Time has become my enemy.

November 7, 1976

I called Mom today and told her about the pregnancy. She's beside herself and in a great deal of pain, but I can't do anything for her, and that makes me so sad. I can't undo anything that's been done. I can't tell her I was raped. She hung up on me, something she's never done. Now maybe I don't have anyone in San Francisco anymore either. Maybe I don't have a mom.

After I hung up, I just sat in the breakfast nook. I have no options. I'm having such disturbing thoughts, and I'm afraid of what I might do to myself. I just don't want to live anymore. What for? It seems as if around every corner, there are more surprises. I don't know how much more I can take.

November 11, 1976

I called Rob today. I don't want to go back to him. I've tried for the last couple of months to write to him about the pregnancy, and while talking to him today, it finally slipped out. I'd had it. But it's finally out to both of them, he and my mom. I told him not to get upset, that I had something to tell him. He got really quiet; he sounds so different to me now anyway, I'm never sure of his mood or what he's going to say.

Anyway, I told him that I didn't want to talk about how it happened but that I had become pregnant while in Michigan. That it was a mistake, but that it was too late to do anything about. I can't tell him I was raped; he'd kill the man. But I don't want him to think the worst of me. He was starting to accuse me of being with everyone. How can I get him to believe that I've never been to bed with anyone, ever? It's better to let him think it was someone out here, I suppose. He's certainly not going to come out here. I can't tell him the truth, though, and that makes me sad, because I don't have anyone at all to tell. No one in the world.

And then it happened again. Those thoughts. The thoughts that tell me there's no way out. That I'm trapped. That even though I got out of the house, I'm still not free and I never will be. I walked over to the sink and looked out at the yard below. It was late afternoon by then, dark and rainy, and several children were splashing in the puddles. I was running out of time. I looked to my left at the knives on the counter. One swift slice. One straight, strong slice across my stomach, and it would be over. I picked up the largest one and felt the blade with my thumb. I couldn't hear the children outside anymore, just my breathing.

I was wearing a shirt I had bought yesterday. It was soft and pink and baggy, with plenty of room still to grow, and it had a little kitten playing with a mama cat and the word MOM written across the chest.

I pulled the shirt up over my stomach and passed my hand over it, feeling her body inside me. She was quiet. Sleeping. I pressed the knife into my skin, making an impression. I remember telling myself to pull my hand back, quick. Quick. Quick. I'm not sure how long I stood there, my heart pounding, my skin on fire, until I felt her move inside me. She saved my life.

I sank to the floor and became so sick I couldn't move. I tried to stand up to go to the bathroom, but I just couldn't make it. I just lay on my side like in the bathroom that day.

January 17, 1977

It feels good to be back in my kitchen. Back in my home. I was surprised when Rob picked me up at the airport. I'm not sure how he figured out what flight I'd be on or exactly when I was coming in. Maybe he called Lisa and got the flight information. I wanted to be alone for a couple of days when I got back. I don't want to see anybody.

I hardly recognized him when I saw him. He kind of scared me, the way he looked. His pupils were dilated and looked huge and black. He had huge, brown bags under his eyes as if he hadn't slept for weeks. And he looked thinner than he had when I left. Other than that, physically he looked okay, but something was different about him. He seemed on edge, and he kept looking around. And when we turned to go, he grabbed hold of my elbow really hard and kept pressing into my skin tighter and tighter.

Bill was waiting in the Jeep outside. He and Rob suggested that we go back to the hotel, but I asked him to take me home instead. I was tired and just wanted to lie down. I had so much to think about and so much to arrange, but I was exhausted.

At first, on the ride home from the airport, Rob couldn't keep his eyes on me; he was so restless and fidgety. Then he wouldn't take his eyes off me. Finally I just told him to please quit staring at me. He said we needed to talk and that he was upset about the baby, and asked me what I was going to do. I told him that we should talk later, and he seemed okay with it, but I really didn't think it was any of his business. I was trying to handle this on my own.

When he took me to the door, he moved his face toward me to give me a kiss, but I sort of backed away. I have to change my life now. It's different than when I left. I'm a different person. I feel like I went through a lot, and I have to take care of myself now. I have to do what's best for me.

When I turned around to go, he grabbed my elbow and turned me around. He pushed me against the door and fell against my stomach. He took my face into his hand and kissed my mouth. This can't go on. I have to change this, but I don't know how. I can't think about it right now.

I got a chill when I put my key in the door. The last time I did that, I was getting home after the rape. At least, I think I did it that day. I must have. I wouldn't have found myself in the shower if I hadn't let myself in but . . . I just don't remember. I can't believe what's happened to me since then. I just can't believe it. I had a flash of how my clothes looked in a pile outside my bedroom door. I can't help crying, being here. It brings it all back, but it's my apartment; where else am I going to go? Maybe that's one of the things I can do . . . move. But there are just so many other things I have to do right now.

My kitchen feels warm and safe. My plants. My music. My books. If I stay here forever, if I never move from this spot, I'll be fine. All my energy is draining out of me as I sit here. Everything . . . I just kept myself going and going and going and now . . . I just want to stop. I'm tired.

January 19, 1977

It's colder than I ever remember it being in San Francisco, but I'm glad to be here, away from Michigan. Walking around the city, though, exploring the hidden alleys full of luscious smells and intriguing sites . . . that's gone to me now. Fear has taken the place of my sense of adventure. It feels like only days have gone by since the rape. My physical injuries are almost healed, but the emotional ones are as fresh as the day it happened.

I'm avoiding the area around the house where it happened. Two blocks have become four that I won't travel into, four have become six, six have become eight. My home has become my prison. I wonder about the man all the time. Where is he now? Has he hurt someone else? And I'm dying from this guilt. I should have done something before, but everything happened so fast and then Daddy died. I was in shock.

I made an appointment with a nearby hospital the day before yesterday, as soon as I got home. I told a nurse on the phone that I was unmarried, seven months and a week pregnant, and that I wanted adoption information. She sounded downright thrilled that I had called. She said they had plenty of couples waiting for healthy newborns. Another pang of guilt. How healthy will she be? I decided I'd talk to her in person, and was just happy to have found someone I thought was going to help me. Returning to the church.

The smell of age and illness in the building overwhelmed me. The nurse met me at the top of the stairs. I was surprised that she still wore a habit and looked much more severe than she had sounded on the phone. I couldn't imagine her giving me an exam, and I wanted to get out of there right away. I wasn't sure this was the place I was supposed to be. Would they take good care of my baby? Would I get good care here?

The nun-nurse had me wait in the lobby until my admissions card was prepared and she'd take me to the delivery room and explain how labor and delivery would go, and then how we (we?) would turn over the baby to the couple who was adopting it (it?).

The wait was endless, and I started tearing up several times. All I wanted was out. Out of this building. Out of this situation. Out of these memories. Out. I'm giving away a child that's coming out of my body. Suddenly the nun-nurse was in front of me again. Looking in my eyes with the card in one hand and her other outstretched, she calmly asked for the $500. $500?

"Oh yes, dear. You were told on the phone that we need the $500 up front to begin the adoption process." No. No one told me that I had to pay to give up my baby. I just assumed . . . I just assumed that I could get help there. Haven't I paid enough? She might as well have said $50,000 or $500,000. How was I going to get $500?

I want to jump off a building. I really do. Rob took me up to the roof and I got close to the edge, and I wanted to jump off. I know I'm going to have to deliver the baby, and I'm scared to death. I think I'll give the rattle and the bibs to the couple who are going to adopt her. I wonder what they'll be like. What an odd thing to do, giving them the gifts I bought her. As if giving them a child wasn't enough. I want to remain a part of her.

I'm going to have to find another adoption agency. I'm thinking about calling Dr. Whitman. It's been a long time, but maybe he can help me.

January 20, 1977

I'm scared that this is more than I can handle emotionally. I feel numb, as if I'm being sucked into a swirling whirlpool. As if my destiny has been determined.

I'm not going to tell the adoptive couple how she was conceived. Am I doing a bad thing? I'm doing it for my sake, not theirs. I don't want to relive what happened, and I *can't confide in anyone, particularly strangers. The sooner this is over, the better. Still, I don't feel like I'm being honest. Well, I'm really not being honest, though, am I?*

No matter how I justify it in my mind, I know it's wrong if I don't tell them. They have a right to know. I'm afraid if anyone knows how she was conceived, they won't want her. How can I take care of her? How can I look in her eyes? I'm petrified. No matter how I turn the situation over in my mind, I'm trapped. I don't know who the rapist was; all I know is his behavior on that day. I know what he's capable of, nothing more. Will she suffer from mental problems? Physical? Emotional? Is it fair to the couple who will adopt her to keep this from them? No. Can I live with no one wanting her and having to raise her by myself? No. I just don't know what to do.

January 24, 1977

It's 12:30 in the morning, so I guess it's really January 25. I can't sleep. I feel like if I go to sleep, I'm not going to wake up. I have to get up at 5:30 to get to the hospital at 6:30, and my stomach is really starting to hurt. I feel like I'm leaving part of myself behind tonight. Like tomorrow after this is all over, I'm not going to be a young girl anymore. Like I'm going to have an experience that a woman has and that I'm going to be different.

Rob came to pick me up earlier this evening to go for a walk. I told him earlier that I didn't want to go, that I didn't feel well and that I had to go to the hospital early tomorrow morning, but he came over anyway and he brought some friends. I hate it when he does this. I feel like I'm being manipulated into doing something I don't want to do.

We walked to the hill overlooking the Pyramid. I felt as if I were moving in slow motion. I knew I shouldn't be out, the pain in my stomach and back were beginning to get sort of intense. The city was a carpet of shining diamonds laid out before us. San Francisco is my home, but I feel so lost. It seems it'll never hold the wonder for me that it once had.

Rob reached for my hand, but I drew back from him. I don't want to be touched by anyone. I resisted the urge to raise my voice to him to just, please, leave me alone. Rob mistook my trembling for a cold chill and tried to put his arms around me, but I pulled back pretty violently from him and turned away. I'm so frightened. His touch is like a vise around me. I was surprised to taste blood in my mouth where I ripped off a piece of skin from my lip. It tastes so familiar to me now. I couldn't hold my tears back. They felt hot on my cheeks. Rob got angry when he saw me crying, and turned back to the others.

A hundred times today, I pulled the sheet of paper Dr. Whitman gave me out of my purse. The paper's creased and torn, and I held onto it like a lifeline. Since the rape, I've had no idea of what tomorrow will bring, but now my tomorrow, or seventy-two hours anyway, are spelled out for me. As long as I don't have a seizure, go into a coma, or die. God help me, what am I doing? What makes me think that God is going to help me now?

The paper says:

Labor Induction Procedure: Your physician will inject a saline solution into the amniotic sac through the abdomen, which will cause expulsion of the fetus through your uterus. Known as a "saline abortion," this procedure is used in pregnancy after sixteen weeks when enough fluid has accumulated in the amniotic fluid sac surrounding the baby. A needle is inserted through your abdomen, and 50-250 ml of amniotic fluid is withdrawn and replaced with a solution of concentrated salt. The fetus will cease movement, usually within four to five hours and will be delivered within 72 hours. You will experience labor and should be aware of serious side effects on the central nervous system. Seizures, coma, or death may result.

I'm so scared. What if I die? Why did I live through everything in that house to have to go through this? The lapidary Dr. Whitman put in this morning is getting difficult to ignore. It's bringing tears to my eyes. I told Rob I wasn't feeling well and needed to come home, but I had to wait out a couple of contractions on my way down the hill. I was afraid maybe I wouldn't make it. They said that it wouldn't start hurting really bad until I was in the hospital, but this is getting pretty painful. It feels good to lie down, but there aren't many positions that are comfortable any more.

I love looking down to Polk Street. The perfect view. I never get tired of looking out the window.

Shit. These aren't contractions, labor or . . . That was a tough one. I wonder if everything is all right. Is this the way I'm supposed to feel? Stan at Princess Market asked me how I was feeling. So sweet. No one's really been intrusive. I almost wish someone would be; I'd love to talk to someone, but I don't feel comfortable bringing it up myself, and they probably don't want to seem nosy, so no one says anything about this big thing that's staring everyone in the face. Anyway, I wish I could tell someone what's happening to me, but even Stan . . . when am I supposed to talk to him, in between customers? And he's not really a close friend.

God . . . they said the contractions were going to be like having my period, but they're getting really strong. It feels like someone's twisting my insides. I can't get comfortable.

When I lie on my back and a contraction comes, I feel like I can see the baby move up off my tummy. I won't have her inside me tomorrow. I wish I could hold someone's hand . . .

Phil's knock on the bathroom door brought me around. I hadn't realized the tears were streaming down my cheeks as I read the journal, or how cold the water had become. That period in my life had been all but lost to me. I'd pushed it from my mind, and my heart, with a vengeance.

"Are you okay, baby?" Phil called through the door.

"Yeah . . . please . . . come in . . . I was just reading some of my journal," I called back and started to get out of the water, throwing the journal off to the side. Phil was, is, the least intrusive person I've ever met. He respects my privacy completely and, while he always lets me know he's there for me no matter what, he never pushes. I looked in his beautiful brown eyes. They held my world. And he held my heart.

He grabbed a thick terrycloth robe from behind the door and wrapped it around me, pulling my hair from the back. He wrapped his arms around me, and I was safe again. Not a scared young girl on the eve of delivering a stillborn baby, not a naive young girl trapped inside a house on a musty, smelly mattress being raped, but in his arms I was someone who mattered.

Without a word, he walked me into the bedroom and laid me on the bed. And when we made love, it was with the passion of someone who had been imprisoned for a very long time. And with the orgasm came release from everything.

Later that night, or maybe early the next morning, when I awoke and couldn't fall back to sleep, as I listened to the waves break on the rocks outside our room, I thought about the evening in my apartment before going to the hospital. The journal brought it all back in penetrating detail . . .

Before long, the pain had become too intense to even write. I lay down on my side and looked out the window toward the corner. My bedroom afforded me the perfect view. I never tired of the sights, the smells, the sounds of Polk Street. The sweet aroma of the bakery mixed with the pungent smells of a Chinese restaurant. The men, some dressed like women, visited with friends and partied into the night. I longed for the freedom they enjoyed. They lived in a world which accepted them . . . a privilege, to be sure. These were my friends, yet I could let none of them in.

A wracking contraction tore me from my thoughts. For a moment, I thought of calling Dr. Whitman to see if something was wrong, or if this was going to continue through the night, but thought better of the idea. In any case, his disapproval of me that morning, the momentary look of disappointment that crossed his face and hung in his eyes, still stung me.

"You were supposed to come back. I told you to come back so we could discuss surgery." His admonition made me angry. How dare he assume that he knew me, knew my pain, knew what I was going through.

It passed quickly, though. He had always given me excellent care, and even my momentary anger at him made me ashamed. He deserved a reason for my not returning. And besides, I was tired. Tired of pretending the rape didn't happen, tired of keeping all this bottled up inside me.

"I . . . I . . . was assaulted and . . . Daddy was killed. I've . . . been away . . . "

Months of pain poured out of me. Sobbing, I dropped my head into my hands. I immediately felt sorry that I'd opened my mouth. He didn't deserve to have this dropped in his lap. So desperate was my need to talk to him, to someone, about what had happened. I hadn't realized until that moment how fresh the pain still was. I was shaking uncontrollably.

My body tensed slightly when he put his arms around me and lay my head against his chest. I was so uncomfortable with touching . . . he let me cry for several more minutes and refrained from asking me any further questions. But when he pulled my chin up to look in my face, his eyes told me that he understood my pain and shared with me, if only for a moment, my despair.

"She's gotten so quiet inside me in the last couple of days. So still. Her stillness makes me feel so alone. I keep waiting for her to move and . . . then . . . then another small movement. I feel so sick. And the bleeding . . . it's different. Then the rape. Then Daddy. Please . . . tell me everything's okay."

My words poured from me in a long sentence with no breath until he moved back from me and gently placed his hands on my shoulders to calm me.

He helped me lie back on the examining table. He was more gentle than usual, and I was grateful for the time he took rubbing my thighs in order to relax me. This was my first exam since the rape. I hadn't even had one at the clinic when I found out I was pregnant . . . I left too soon. I felt so vulnerable and open, as if he could see all that had happened to me. I was no longer a virgin. No longer clean. His approval, his acceptance of me as a worthy person became paramount.

I fought the urge to simply babble on and on as he went about his exam. I wanted him to see that the rape had not changed me and that it was nothing. That I was the same young woman that I had always been. But it had changed me. I was not the same.

It was difficult . . . it still is . . . for me to lie on my back since the rape. Images come to me. As he was examining me, I felt a heaviness on my chest, like when the man brought his hand down around my neck. Breathing always became difficult in this position, and I was anxious for the exam to be over. He inserted his fingers in me and pressed against my abdomen, causing me to catch my breath. My eyes closed and I relaxed, hoping it would make the rest of the exam easier. He withdrew his fingers and absent-mindedly circled my stomach, warming me. His manner became crisp and measured.

"Get the hospital on the phone," he called to his nurse, shouting several other instructions for further tests as she walked out the door. When he turned to me, his face was once again gentle. "I'm sorry, Teresa. I'm going to have to take the baby now, if we're to take care of you." He must have seen the stunned look on my face, because he quickly explained. He needed to do surgery right away, and the procedure would seriously compromise being able to move forward with the pregnancy. The baby was in serious distress and I was in danger.

"I'm not due yet," I stammered. "How are you going to do this? Can you do this?" Things were moving at lightning speed around me. While I begged for someone to end this pregnancy months ago, it was too late now. I had a million questions. "How is the baby going to live at this stage? Is she okay? Has something happened to her?"

He became quiet. The whole room grew quiet. My heart pounded in my ears, and I bit my lip hard enough to draw blood. Someone say something, I wanted to scream. Tell me this isn't happening.

Someone lowered me down on my back again. Too fast. This is happening too fast. I can't think. I need time to think. Dr. Whitman left the room for a moment, and the nurse came around my right side, helping me put my legs in the stirrups. I felt my head float to the pillow on the table and looked up at the poster on the ceiling. It was a photograph of tiny, baby butterflies. Babies.

Dr. Whitman came back in the room, moving his chair in close between my legs. In one deft motion, his hand was inside me, inserting something.

"This will be over in a couple of days, Teresa," he said, reaching for my hands. He held them for a moment and looked into my eyes. The pounding in my ears barely allowed me to make sense of his words. I heard myself responding to his questions. Yes,

I'll be at the hospital tomorrow morning. Yes, I have someone to come with me. Yes, I'll be fine . . .

No . . . no . . . I wanted to yell at his back as he walked from the room, please don't leave me. Susan, a counselor that he had called from up front, took me back out to a dreary little room full of pictures of babies in various stages. More babies.

"You're really far along." She kept her eyes on my stomach and rarely brought them up to meet mine. I tried to swallow my fear, to form the questions running through my mind into some sort of coherent sentence, but I couldn't.

She explained that I'd be experiencing the lapidary starting to work soon. It would start as cramps. I should get a lot of rest. I shouldn't eat much tonight, and I shouldn't go anywhere but home, and I would have to check into the hospital at 6:30 a.m.

"Oh, and bring a magazine . . . it's going to take a long time . . . "

I remember glancing back at the clock on my dresser. 2:30 a.m. Sleep didn't come, the contractions were so intense and the night was so long.

I looked at Phil sleeping next to me. His soft breath blew against my skin, and his chest rose and fell ever so slightly. The indentation he made in the bed was almost imperceptible for such a tall, large man. I felt so sorry for all I'd put him through, for all the years that I spent in isolation. Not talking about my feelings. Not telling him what was wrong when the pain became too much for me. He never understood my wanting to retreat. My feelings of being trapped into a corner and what I'd do to avoid those feelings. He'd been there for me always, my savior in the most true sense.

It had been a year since I started therapy, and I was in pain. There really was no other way to describe it. There were times when I didn't want to face the rape, the birth, the infertility, all of it. The aftermath of those fourteen hours. Lying there next to Phil early that morning, I realized that I was doing it, *am* doing it, for him. For us. For our marriage.

I'd brought the white envelope with me to Bodega Bay. I thought for a moment of getting up and reading it, but the darkness seemed like an enemy. It would be better to wait until the following day, when it was sunny and the world was right-side-up again.

Chapter 10

January, 1996

"I'm sorry I hurt you."

The pain of what Gary said must have registered on my face, but his question was intuitive and caught me off-guard.

Yes, I answered him, she was a child to me, and yes I had named her. I feel, I went on to tell him, like a pathetic mother animal who has lost her child and is searching for her baby. The pain of the rape is ripped fresh again each year when I think of her birth. And each year I re-negotiate with myself. Right versus wrong. Good versus evil. My anger that I was forced into an impossible position was intense and unending. My agony lingered.

"You're right . . . I feel I'm inherently *bad*. I was a *bad* girl, and now I'm a *bad* woman. I'm choking under the weight of it. I guess I feel guilty. Guilty for everything: my parents, the baby. But your words . . . your words are very comforting to me." I lowered my eyes.

Reading my journal brought back powerful emotions. Gary sensed that the issue was an important one that needed to be addressed, but I backed away. His gentle persuasion, though, his knowing when to push and when to back away made me feel safe and eventually willing to talk. And so, I told him the story of Sarah's birth . . .

The sheets, newly cleaned and pressed, felt cold against my skin. I already had a slight fever, the admitting nurse told me, which I suppose made the sheets seem even more chilly. I was shaking as the orderly laid me back on the bed. A flurry of activity went on around me in the room . . . one nurse took my blood pressure while another told me the doctor would be right in.

Dr. Whitman's sober mood was contagious. The room grew quiet when he entered, and everyone went about their work. I'd been looking forward to seeing him again, but he seemed . . . changed. He was businesslike as he took the solution from a nurse and shouted several other orders. I realized that this was probably very difficult for him also. The orderlies left the room, leaving the four of us alone.

He helped me move to the bottom of the bed so he could reach me more easily, and held my hands for a moment as he had the day before. Spreading my legs, he examined me while the nurses, one on each side of me, took my hands. Stunned, I realized they were bringing them above my head and securing them to the bed rails. Just like the rape, I was tied and constricted . . . and panicking. My heart beat loudly in my ears. I tried to speak but couldn't, just like the rape.

No one spoke. The nurses held onto my arms as I clutched the bed rail, petrified at what was going to happen. Moments seemed like hours. I looked up at the nurse to my right. She avoided my eyes, but I kept looking at hers. I recall them now; they were brown and large and warm. Please look at me while you're doing this, I wanted to say. Please don't make me feel as if I'm not here.

The doctor felt along my pubic bone, came up slightly into my abdomen, and began inserting the needle. Painstakingly, he started emptying the solution into me. The steel beneath my hand was cold. I held on tightly and ached for it to be someone's hand I was holding. The pain was agonizing. Slow . . . slow torture. My fingernails dug into the palms of my hands; the skin pulled taut over my knuckles. I closed my eyes and tried to manage the pain but saw lights throbbing behind them.

Dr. Whitman pushed against my abdomen, trying to keep me still as my back arched. The stab was more intense as he pushed the needle against me, emptying the contents. Carefully pulling the needle back out, he rubbed a burning solution onto my skin as the nurses untied my hands. As soon as the needle emptied, I wanted to scream at the doctor to pull it out. Make it stop. Make the pain of the rape just go away. I so desperately needed someone to hold me. I craved warmth, but felt raw and open.

I rolled onto my left side as they spoke to me, bringing my legs up and holding my stomach. Their words became more and more faded. I was exhausted and wanted someone to take care of me. I just didn't want to think about anything anymore. The past seven and a half months had been hell, and it would soon be over.

One of the nurses covered me with a warm blanket, turned off the lights, and I was alone. A soft, misty sleep came over me . . . that place between being asleep and being awake. The contractions hadn't subsided but were manageable, particularly compared to the distress the needle had caused. I felt flushed, feverish, and started having fragmented, disconcerting dreams. Dreams of babies and death, and horrible feelings and thoughts. Words jelled and then became porous, dissipating before I could make them out.

Thrashing inside me tore me from my sleep. A terrible, thrashing inside me. The contractions were still not terribly strong, making this sensation even more haunting. Hugging my stomach, I sat and cried for what seemed like hours. My dream of a child one day . . . of a family . . . I felt as if it was slipping away. It was still dark, and I wanted to turn the lights on, but couldn't move. Didn't want to move. I was so afraid at what was happening.

My mom and Rob had came to the hospital with me, but I hadn't seen them yet. Things were terrible between Rob and I, even worse than before I went to Michigan, but I was glad when he said he'd come with me. I needed someone here with me.

I had come in at 6:30 and wondered how late it was. I reached over to my left, feeling along the cold wall, but I couldn't find a buzzer for the nurse, so I just lay back, holding my stomach, feeling the baby's life tear from me. The thrashing inside me was unbelievable. Trying to breathe through what contractions there were, as well as control my breathing for her flailing about, became impossible. I knew she was dying, and suddenly I couldn't breathe any longer. I brought air into my lungs without being able to release any. Someone, a human being, was dying inside me. I was inconsolable. My life had turned out so differently than I thought it would only eight months ago. I wanted to die. No one came in to check on me.

Stretching my legs out, I leaned back on my hands, trying to ease the tumult going on inside me. The light snapped on, wrenching me from my dazed state. A nurse came in and asked me to lie back, telling me that she was going to examine me and that several other doctors would be in as well. Tears rolled down my face as she inserted her fingers inside me. Images . . . flashbacks of the rape . . . flooded me. I was on my back again with a stranger putting their fingers inside me. The doctors came in and spoke with each other as if I wasn't there, but Dr. Whitman wasn't with them. I was surrounded by strangers inserting their hands inside me, checking the size of my cervix, pressing against my stomach and abdomen. Feeling the storm inside me.

They congregated in the corner and started talking about "the case." One of the doctors asked an older one a question. "Couldn't she have the child . . . ?" I heard in a vague whisper. They were discussing me as if I were a piece of meat, not a human being. "Does she know that . . . ?" I strained to hear the rest of what he was saying. I was growing angry that they wouldn't just talk to me directly. "I saw signs of . . ." Again, I was unable to hear the rest.

The baby took five and a half hours to die following the injection. It was a violent, raw death. Her end didn't come easily. She held on and I held on. For hours, she tossed about inside me. Where yesterday there was barely any movement, today it seemed she'd move around inside me forever. And for hours I cried. Until there was just . . . nothing. One moment just . . . nothing. No more, and again I was alone. An eerie stillness came over me as her last movement subsided. It seemed my spirit, my essence, just slipped away with her. All the struggles to get out of the house, for what? To feel my child die inside me? To endure all this pain?

For hours I cried. I knew the pain, the physical pain, the emotional pain, was only just beginning. My body took on a rhythm all its own after she died. The contractions began in earnest; my body was desperate to release her from it, yet just as desperate to hold onto her. The power behind the pain surprised me, and I tried repeatedly to resist the temptation to tense up.

I needed someone to be with me, to help me breathe through these incredible sensations. I wanted to walk around but was too exhausted to move. The contractions were strong and low down in my back, reaching around my hips into my abdomen. I felt as if someone had sliced me open with a sharp knife from my pubic bone to my belly button. In the chaos, I saw images of my muscles being pulled back and back . . . out . . . out to the sides and laid out perpendicular to my abdomen. Someone, I was sure, was taking these long muscles and bringing them around my back, twisting them into a knot. Bizarre images overtook me.

It was an intense effort bringing forth this baby. I tried to imagine scenes outside of me, but became scared. The birth of this baby was becoming more like the rape every moment . . . the feeling of being trapped . . . of not knowing what pain was coming . . .

I wanted the nurse, the doctor, someone, to hold my hand, and I reached out to them as they walked toward the door. The screams of the other women were driving me nuts. I didn't want to hear them. I didn't want to hear their husbands yelling, "Hold on, honey! I love you, honey!"

Hours went by like this. I'd lie on one side, then the other, trying to get comfortable. The rhythm wasn't regular, and I was concerned that something was wrong. It was wrong for the baby to be inside me for this long . . . it was dead . . . I had to get it out. I couldn't regulate my breathing enough to work with the contractions instead of against them. My mom and Rob finally appeared and stood there looking at me. Just staring. Why didn't they come over to me? Why didn't they say something . . . hold me . . . help me? I turned my back toward them.

Dr. Whitman grew concerned. It was difficult for me to hear him, to comprehend what he was saying to me. My eyes tried to focus, but the pain was relentless. Struggling to make me understand, he held my head in his hands and looked deep into my eyes, trying to calm me for a moment. I'd already been there for thirty hours, he told me, and something might be wrong. The pain I told the nurse that I was experiencing — I didn't even remember talking to the nurse — was signaling that something might be wrong, so they were going to bring in an x-ray machine.

Soon a large machine appeared in the room, nearly taking all the space. Move here . . . this way . . . no, this way . . . the technician was trying to take an image, but every movement was agony.

"No," the nurse answered my begging for medication, "you can't have any." As if I'd been bad. How can she do that, I wondered? How can she answer questions locked away inside me? Questions I haven't even asked. The technician finally took the image and said the doctor would be in to speak with me.

Time was no longer measurable to me. I had no idea how long I'd been there . . . how long it had been since Dr. Whitman was in . . . nothing. I had no conception of time. I thought I might ask someone for a watch, but decided against it. Everything outside my eyes was a blur, in any case. Tears filled them. Dr. Whitman finally returned with my x-ray. He said that I had broken my tailbone sometime in the past, and it had never healed.

"How did that happen?" he asked me. I replied that I wasn't sure, but the moment he said it, I knew. The man had turned me over and sodomized me. I knew it was while he was doing that; I'd felt a snap and a bolt of pain that reached way into my back. I'd had a great deal of pain since then . . . sitting . . . standing . . . walking. Tears pooled around my eyes; I wanted to be left alone.

Dr. Whitman moved around to the foot of the bed and started talking to the nurse, too low again for me to hear. They'd have to . . . and how about the . . . be careful not to . . . cesarean was out of the question . . .

Tell me! I wanted to yell. Tell me what to do! How do I get this baby out of me? She's dead . . . don't drag it out any longer than you have to.

Dr. Whitman came back and put his hand on my shoulder. "Teresa . . . we just can't do a cesarean . . . you have to handle this. I'm sorry. Even though you're going to feel an overwhelming urge, don't push." And with that, he was gone. I was glad to be alone again. This was taking an incredible amount of energy from me, and seeing anyone else — particularly my mom — just made me feel as if I couldn't let on how I felt. I didn't want her to see me in pain. I didn't want to hurt her.

Minutes turned into hours. The physical pain that wracked my body was an excuse, a justification to cry out, but still I could not. My anger turned inside me as the reticence to express my pain became more and more a part of me. Everything was progressing slowly, ever so slowly.

Dr. Whitman estimated another ten hours or so, and I felt like giving up. *Ten hours? He might as well have said a hundred hours . . . I can't do this. Let's just give it up right now and go home.* My body was shutting down, not cooperating with the rhythm of the contractions. *I was fighting losing her forever, yet I knew I had to get her outside of my body. Just rip her out.*

A nurse came in to examine me. "Let it out, honey. Cry. Scream. This is the one time you're allowed." Even with her words, I couldn't. *How could she understand? How could anyone? To cry out while I was being raped meant I might be killed. I couldn't then . . . and I couldn't now.*

I grabbed her hand as she turned to leave. "Please . . . please . . . make this go away. Please give me something."

Her eyes grew warm, but she had an edge to her voice. "Honey, just concentrate. I can't give you anything. I'm sorry."

Rob came in shortly after she left and sat staring at me. I turned over on my left side, working through the contractions. *Trying to remember what the book had said about breathing . . . breathe through . . . no . . . hold your breath here . . . no . . . When the hell did I breathe and when the hell did I not? I just wanted this pain to be over.*

I had nearly forgotten that Rob was in the room when he moved over to me and leaned against the bed. I felt the pressure of his hand on my shoulder as he leaned toward me, putting his mouth next to my ear. My eyes closed, and my body relaxed ever so slightly. His nearness felt good. *I needed his hands on me. I needed him to help me do this.* He was so close that his breath brushed against my ear.

"I only wanted Mark to scare you. This is an added bonus."

A wall of white with blue lights slammed into my face. A huge contraction shook me at just that moment. I felt his hand come up off my shoulder and heard him walk from the room. I saw nothing in front of me. My breath stopped. What? What? Everything swam in front of my eyes . . . the fourteen hours of hell the man put me through . . . What? You're saying what? I tried to turn to look at him, but was in excruciating pain, and he'd already left in any case.

My left hand was clutching the steel bed rail, and my other was gripping the sheet. My knuckles turned white and my fingernails dug into the palms of my hands. I began shaking uncontrollably. Between the incredible rage and the contractions, I felt as if I was going to explode. My head throbbed so bad I thought I was going to have a stroke. How could he have done this to me? Everything went black.

When I awoke — I'm not sure how much later — I was shivering . . . cold . . . hot . . . I wasn't sure what I was feeling. Everything was spinning around me. I was still lying on my side. I tried to straighten my elbow and raise up on my left hand, when I felt the baby's head push against my cervix. I screamed for a nurse, the only time I can remember raising my voice.

Incredible. What an incredible feeling. I felt shaky and weak and alone, but knowing it would be over gave me some strength. The nurses came in telling me that the doctor was out of the building. I don't care where he is, I thought, this baby is coming out whether he's here or not.

The contractions were unbearable. My breath caught in and in and in without exhaling. The pressure against my cervix was astounding. I didn't want anyone with me. Now I wanted to scream to everyone to leave me alone and let me do this. I felt like kneeling on my hands and knees to relieve the pressure, but there was no room on the bed.

An incredible rush came over me as her head moved through my pelvic bones. I could actually feel her head making its way through my body. The need to push was incredible, but there were people telling me not to. The doctor finally arrived, and everyone made room for him between my legs. He spread my legs further apart and moved himself closer to me, putting his hand against me as she moved lower. Some kind of force was moving through me.

The feeling of her half-in and half-out of me was astounding. Tears streamed from my eyes. Each contraction brought a tremendous urge to push, but with each contraction I felt her recede a little into me. Orders to bear down . . . to push. The doctor brought my knees up closer to my chest and told me to pull tight. I thought I was going to the delivery room, but realized that he was going to deliver the baby right there. I grabbed onto his arm.

"Aren't we going to . . . ?"

He knew what I was asking. "No," he replied. "We don't do abortions in the delivery room . . . only live births. Concentrate, Teresa . . . we have to get this baby out of you . . . other women who are having babies don't need to see this."

The pain I felt . . . emotional . . . physical . . . mental . . . the pain of his statement. No, of course, a woman having a beautiful baby shouldn't have to see a woman giving birth to a dead one. What was I thinking? This baby is dead. But she's nestled inside me . . . she's safe . . . she's mine. She's not yours yet.

Shaking . . . shivering . . . screaming inside . . . I pushed her out of me. Such tremendous force, like the force of the entire world was within me . . . moving through me. My muscles tightened around her body as she moved through me. I held on tight, the only way I knew how. I reached down and felt her flesh between my legs but could see nothing. I didn't want to let her go. The nurse took the baby from between my legs. Crying . . . sobbing . . . I couldn't stop.

"Please," I begged one of the nurses, "let me see her . . . just for a moment." She ignored my outstretched hands and my pleas to see the baby, and laid her on a small table. I watched as she wrapped her in something. The silence was deafening. I prayed that I would hear her cry . . . something. Please, don't let this happen, I screamed inside. Please . . . don't you know how I've suffered for her . . . don't you know that my suffering will be for nothing?

As one of the nurses and the doctor helped me with contractions to expel the placenta, the other just put her small body in the paper bag and made out a form. Everyone avoided my eyes.

The nurse turned toward me with the bag in her arms. "She has green eyes," she said, and walked past me out the door.

Several days after surgery, I lay in bed on my side and felt my nightgown grow wet beneath me. Alarmed, I sat straight up and pulled it out in front of me. Two large milk stains covered the front of my nightgown and leaked down my front. My body was ready to nurse the baby who had just died. I cried until my eyes hurt. My heart ached so bad . . .

"It still does, even now."

I was exhausted as I sat looking into Gary's eyes. They were comforting and warm, and I needed him. There was nothing more to say; my soul was open to him. And he looked incredibly sad. I suppose his face reflected how very sad I must have looked to him.

The memory of my body during the birth, of it imploring me to work with it, was astounding. The pain, emotional and physical, helped me feel again after the rape, even though it was at the surface and for such a short time. Telling Gary made me feel my body again, and it was an incredible moment of intimacy, sharing this with him.

I was dying inside. I felt as if I was a huge opening into which emotions and feelings and memories poured, without any respite. I had no recourse, no say in the matter. The feelings were coming inside me without my consent.

I ached to tell Phil how I felt, what was happening to me . . . but I couldn't. I was serving a sentence in my self-imposed prison. Phil is my best friend, my lover, the man I want to spend the rest of my life with . . . yet I longed to tell Phil that evening what happened, but I couldn't. I was so afraid he would see how damaged I really was and leave me.

What I couldn't talk to Gary about that day was the news that because I was injured during the rape, I would never be able to conceive again. I'd contracted chlamydia during the rape, and I was told right before my surgery. Another blow. I still remembered the day Phil and I waited in Dr. Trousdale's office for the results of yet another laparoscopy, a procedure to see the extent of damage to my fallopian tubes.

Dr. Trousdale came into the room and, with a sigh, tossed my file onto his desk. He sat down and took off his glasses before speaking to us. I liked him a lot. He was sweet and always optimistic. With his red hair and bow tie, he reminded me of a leprechaun. He provided me with excellent care when I contracted cervical cancer again.

"I'm sorry, Teresa but . . . " he started, but his voice trailed off. I knew what he was going to say. I had heard it before, but it still made my heart ache. I didn't hear what else he said; I just put my face in my hands and started crying. I couldn't accept that I'd never have children.

I couldn't tell Gary. There was something in the way that I had been relating to Gary lately that bothered me. I felt a nagging sense of, disapproval, I suppose, for lack of a better word.

I never asked Gary what he thought of me after telling him about the baby.

Chapter 11

March, 1996

"Do you think the man who raped me was sorry, even for a moment?" I'm not sure why I asked Gary the question. What was the point? I looked around his office, then back at him. He hadn't spoken.

Lately, I'd had images of myself on the mattress, of walking toward myself and becoming exhausted from the long walk, then looking up and seeing myself even further away. I wasn't making any headway and was frustrated from my lack of progress. I was nervous about the upcoming surgery on my jaw, and not very motivated, and it was hard to concentrate on my work. Sort of a perfectionist in my work, I was really bothered by this inability to apply myself to anything but my personal problems. Plus, my obsessive behaviors hadn't really let up. I was still checking and re-rechecking, and re-checking my re-checking. Exhausting.

It was always a mystery to me whether I should bring these things up to Gary. Always a calculated risk. *Is this an issue I can bring up during our hour together, and then push safely back inside and go on with my life after we're finished? Am I able to bring enough of this out to gain some small measure of insight today, or will I be unable to function after I leave?*

As I slipped into my car after leaving the appointment, I realized I'd never gotten the answer to my question. Like so many other questions, there were no answers.

Two days later, I found myself swathed in bandages, barely able to move my head. I saw white in front of my eyes when they opened. A bright, blinding white. And then Dr. Prentice's face. I thought back to when he came over to the pre-surgery area to check on me. I was talking to several women who were also waiting, and he sat down next to me.

"You ready?" he asked with a broad smile, putting his hand on my shoulder.

"Yes . . . yes . . . I'm ready." I was incredibly nervous and had to go to the bathroom, but I was as ready as I would ever be.

After he left, the other women turned toward me with their voices low.

"He's your *doctor*?"

"Boy . . . he's so *handsome!*"

"Yeah . . . where'd you find *him*?"

Their words came back to me in the post-op area where I'd been wheeled. It was hard to move my face, the bandage covering my jaw was so large. He was charming and tall, with salt-and-pepper hair. *If you wanna see someone sexy,* I remember thinking that I should have told them, *you should meet my husband . . . he's eye candy.* Then the pain medication kicked in. My dreams were disorienting, as is typical after surgery. Weird and strange dreams.

This was the second surgery to repair my jaw, and I hadn't been looking forward to it. The first one was difficult, yet hadn't resolved the problem I was having with pain. This was my last hope. Dr. Prentice gave me the news during a follow-up appointment, several weeks earlier.

Suddenly, everything broke like a dam. With Phil on my left and Dr. Prentice on my right, I just lost it and started sobbing. His question was innocent: *Had I been wearing my night guard?*

"I can't wear anything," I said, looking at him. "I can't put anything in my mouth." I hoped he wasn't going to force me any further, but his eyes questioned me. I felt as if he thought I was just being lazy. "He . . . put a cloth inside my mouth, and he tried to have oral sex after . . . " My eyes dropped. Tears were already spilling from them.

Dr. Prentice turned from the counter where he'd been writing in my chart. He knew of the rape, of course, and reached toward me, looking deeply into my eyes. Then he ran his hand along my jaw bone, his tenderness like a drink of water to a parched person.

Since I'd begun therapy, I was finally able to tell my doctors what had happened. While incredibly nervous and halting, my words gradually became easier to say. Each of my doctors listened with compassion and understood my discomfort, usually reaching out to physically touch my arm, to connect with me as if to say they were sorry for what I'd been through. And each time I told one of them and received their kind words, I regretted not having opened up sooner. I'd lived under a rock for far too long.

At the same moment, Phil touched me on my shoulder and moved toward me. They couldn't know, of course, what their support and acceptance meant to me.

Two days after surgery, I was back in our home. Phil had to meet with a client and made me a nest on the couch before he left. A nurturing, calm, reassuring person, he's the best to have around when you're sick. He handed me the shake he'd made, and my journal from the box I'd opened marked *Betrayal*. I was tense and unable to relax and thought I might as well do some reading.

February 12, 1977

It's my birthday today. I feel as if I'm in a spiral. The baby has taken everything from me. I've lost the energy to continue and all hope that my life will ever return to normal. I'm certain that I'll read these words one day and feel as if I was being terribly dramatic, but today I just feel sorry for myself.

Rob's betrayal of me has left me paralyzed. Immobilized. Now I constantly question myself and my interactions with others. Even the most minute conversations are examined and then re-examined. Is that really what she meant to say? What is he saying with his eyes, his behavior? And the answer is always the same . . . stay detached in order not to be hurt again. Paranoia is creeping into all the dark corners of my life. I trust no one. I've stopped caring about myself.

I can't have Rob in my life. I want him dead. How could he do this to me? I didn't do anything wrong. He is suffocating me and will kill me, I'm sure, if I try to do anything. I'm afraid he's going to hurt my mom.

My behavior has changed drastically. I feel moody and unable to control my feelings, unable to dig myself out of this hole. It's only been a few weeks, but I'm lost and in pain, and I can't figure out what to do for myself. I've started to analyze every conversation to the nth degree. I don't understand what I'm doing. My mind tells me this is not good, it's almost paranoid, but I can't seem to help myself. And because of what I'm doing, analyzing every little word, every little nuance of every situation, it's easier to find solace in strangers. In meaningless exchanges that take little effort. I've become a public recluse, keeping to myself except for several well-chosen people who know nothing of what happened.

Going back to how it was, picking up the pieces, is really difficult. I made an appointment with an admissions counselor at UC Berkeley, but didn't go. The self-doubt has returned, plus more. How can I study psychology when I'm so broken? How can I help someone else when I clearly can't help myself? Depression and despair have seeped into my bones. Everywhere I turn, there's another challenge to overcome, and I guess I'm just tired of feeling.

February 14, 1977

God forgive me, but I wish Rob would just . . . die. I can't stand it anymore.

My place of refuge used to be work. Now that's gone. I miss Rick terribly, and my job, and taking photos with him, but how could I go back after lying to him that night? When I told him someone in my family had died, I meant me. A part of me had died. But I wonder about him all the time, and Elaine. But at the same time, I'm angry at them for not finding me, for not rescuing me. Maybe they tried. I hope so.

Mr. Brown came into the bank today. He had a lot of business, so we had lots of time to talk. Three hours altogether. Janie says it's a record, even for Mr. Brown. I'm so flattered when he motions other people in front of him while he's waiting for me to be available. Anyway, today after we were finished, he took my hands in his and thanked me. I told him I was happy to help him, but he said that as an old man, he knew whether a person was being nice to him for him or his money. Our relationship is transitory, I know, but I care for him in a special way. He's fascinating and kind and intelligent and sweet.

When I got back from lunch, there was a huge, beautiful bouquet of flowers. The girls gathered around me and giggled as I opened the card. They'd seen who brought them and were anxious to see the look on me face. "To the girl with the most beautiful smile! Yours always, Tom Brown." How wonderful! Better than a raise! It speaks volumes about how we feel about each other. I gave him a call on my break to thank him and tell him how much they meant to me.

Because I'd called Mr. Brown on my break, I didn't have time to call Rob when he expected. In fact, I completely forgot about him. At five minutes to three, just before closing time, I glanced at the line of customers. My heart stopped when I saw Rob. He'd never come into the bank before, and I was afraid of what he might do. He was looking at the flowers. It was too late to reach for them and move them to the desk behind me. Even if I could, knowing him, he'd think they were from someone who was interested in me, and he would get angry.

He seemed to move toward my window in slow motion. He grabbed the note that I had sitting against the vase. He just looked at me. His eyes were cold and made me scared of what he was going to do. He didn't say a word, but he brought his hand up to the counter again and grabbed the vase and smashed it on the green marble floor. The sound was deafening in the huge rotunda of the bank. Just silence followed. Everyone turned to look at him, then looked at me as he walked out the door.

Mr. Watkins was unlocking the door for other customers who were still in the bank, and Rob walked past him as if nothing had happened. I started crying, right there in front of everyone. I locked my cash drawer and ran around to the front of my window to pick up the vase and flowers, but Mr. Watkins grabbed me by the arm and stood me up. He told me my "services" were no longer needed. That they didn't need this kind of trouble. I told him I understood and that I just wanted to clean up my flowers, but he told me to just leave, not to even bother balancing.

I'm so trapped. Rob's becoming more violent and mean. When I see him, I'm just so frightened of what he's going to do to me. Every time I tell him I want him to leave me alone, he starts threatening me. Telling me he could make it ten times worse than what's already happened. That he could have my mom hurt. Seeing him since the hospital has been pure torture for me.

February 20, 1977

Rob has been calling every day since the incident at the bank. And now he's starting to call my mom and bother her. I'm so afraid for her safety. And mine. I leave early for work and hang around downtown between job interviews. I just make sure I have plenty of change for coffee, but I can't keep doing this. I still don't feel very well from the surgery. Dr. Whitman told me to take it easy, but I have to find another job right away. I thought I could sort of relax into getting over everything, but getting fired because of what Rob did . . . well, I'm back at square one. I'm just so, so tired and I wish I could relax.

And so, I sit here once again, alone. Such a small, insignificant word when one does not suffer from aloneness. But a devastating, haunting word to one who does. Self-pity has claimed me, for which I'm ashamed. There are so many other people in the world who are worse off than me, but all I want to be is someone else.

February 22, 1977

Rob called me yesterday. I had to go with him. I don't have a choice anymore. Yesterday he told me he was going to hurt my mom if I didn't keep seeing him, and last night she was mugged outside her apartment. I don't know if it was someone Rob knew or not. How could I be so stupid? I don't know where to turn. I feel so bad about all of this. If I hadn't gotten involved with him, none of this would have happened. How could I have been so naive? How am I going to get out of this? He said we were going back to the hotel, but instead he started driving toward San Jose and we ended up in some place called Sunol. The house he took me to was beautiful, but I didn't like the people who lived there or were visiting there. Rob said he still had some business to do, and that we'd be spending the night there. I didn't like it at all.

The master bedroom — I suppose it was the master bedroom, anyway — was huge. It had two king-sized beds and a patio door that looked out over the valley. The view was beautiful, with thousands and thousands of twinkling lights. I thought about the people in the houses. They were safe and warm and together. I wondered if any of them felt trapped and scared. I wondered if they had someone in their lives who wouldn't leave them alone.

Rob was still out in the living room or somewhere. Although the woman who showed me the bedroom handed me a robe, I kept my clothes on and turned off the lights. I lay down on top of the covers. I was so tired. Tired. Tired. All I could think about was my appointment with Dr. Whitman. He told me the outlook was pretty good . . . but still, I'm scared. After everything that's happened to my body since last year . . . I'm just so tired. I'm still losing blood from the surgery and don't really feel well enough to be out of bed.

Rob came in at about 2:00 . . . I remember looking at the clock. I tried to remain really still and keep my breathing regular. He took off his shoes and lay down on the bed next to me. I smelled the cologne I'd bought him. Now it's everything I can do not to be sick when I'm near him. He moved closer to me, and the weight of his body on the mattress rolled me closer to him. Still, I tried to act as if I was sleeping. He put his hand on my hip. I wanted to move, to run, to scream, but I remained perfectly silent. How can he not know the hell he put me through? I waited until his breathing became regular and then I relaxed a bit.

A couple came in and lay down on the bed across from us. I was facing the bed, and while I wanted to turn away, I didn't want to turn toward Rob. The moans they were making were difficult to ignore, so I opened my eyes just a bit. The moonlight was shining into the room much more than when I first came in, and it shone against their bodies. They'd taken their clothes off and pulled back the covers and were going to start making love in front of us. I was mesmerized by the shapes of their bodies and the light as it played on them. She was stunning in the moonlight, with long, blonde hair, and he was black, ebony, in this light. The contrast between their bodies was exquisite. Didn't they see us? Or didn't they care? My blood pulsated in my ears.

My jaw ached by the time I put down the journal. I missed Phil desperately. Because I couldn't talk into the phone, he wouldn't be calling me . . . but I needed to see him and touch him. It hurt me that I was in such despair at such a young age.

I picked up the white envelope and read the writing: *DON'T OPEN . . . EVER!* I threw it to the side and gave in to the pain pill Phil had put next to me before leaving. I let the haziness just wash over me.

Chapter

April, 1996

Our room was on the twenty-seventh floor of the hotel.

"I feel like jumping," I said, turning around to face Phil.

"As long as you tell me first so I can stop you," he said, wrapping his arms around me. It seemed like such a small step, but it was a huge one, being able to tell Phil how I felt at the moment I was feeling it. And I was right, in a sense: I did still feel like jumping, but it didn't last as long as it had before, and it didn't have the depth that it once had. Now, I knew I wouldn't. I had too much to lose.

The rain gently fell against the huge picture windows. We were in downtown Seattle atop a high hill that afforded a magnificent view of the city and points beyond. I'd learn what they were later, but at that moment, all I wanted to do was talk about my appointment with Gary. We went down to the restaurant on the mezzanine. It was warm and cozy. We sat next to the window and watched as people came in on buses from the airport. The inside was like a small bistro, and the outside had a lot of character with small gaslight lamps.

"Tell me," Phil said, taking my hands. "Tell me what happened on Friday . . . "

And so, I told him what I'd told Gary . . .

I was laboring under misconceptions. About myself, about others. The realization was profound. How had I allowed this to happen? How had I taken everything that happened and turned it against myself? More importantly, how could I change these misconceptions? They were now a part of me. A part of my beliefs.

After learning that Rob had had me raped (the words are still excruciating to read on the page), I tried to recover. I tried to save what self-esteem I had left with actions that I could accomplish.

It was almost three months after the birth. The room in San Francisco where one looks up property records is imposing. Very intimidating, and it took me several visits just to get the nerve to talk to the clerk. It was in late March or early April before I finally got the courage to look for the owner of the house where I was raped. I was haunted by Rob's statement to me in the hospital, and couldn't relax until I knew the truth. Had this been an incredibly horrible joke on me? Or had he really had me raped? Or maybe the pain was so bad I had imagined what I heard. I was afraid to talk to him at all, and avoided him if I could. I always made sure there were other people around us. I still couldn't believe that someone would do this to me.

"I'm looking for a house . . . I mean, an owner of a house . . . in San Francisco." I was sure that someone was watching me, that someone would tell the owner that I was snooping and . . . I tried to grab hold of myself and calm down.

"Address." It was more a statement than a question. "Address!" The man looked at me with disdain from over his round, black-framed glasses.

"Ummm . . . " I pulled the sheet of paper from my skirt pocket.

Several weeks earlier, the only time I'd gone close to the house, I wrote down the address. I was terrified that day, and even more terrified now to be getting close to finding out the truth. I remember working my way up to going past the house; it took several weeks for that too. Each day I would resolve to get the address, and each day there was something that I let get in the way. It was raining. It was sunny. It was too early. It was too late. Until finally, I ran out of excuses.

I walked quickly past the house from across the street, not daring to look for fear the man who had raped me was nearby. I felt dread to my bones, being so close to the house again, and was afraid I would scream. I wanted to. I wanted to scream like I couldn't that day. It was horrible. But after several more walks past it, I had the address. I stood not far from the bushes where he had pushed me down, and looked at the house.

It was as it was that day, not even a year ago. A house of true horror. The tasseled shades were drawn on the first floor, and it seemed quiet. A shiver ran up my spine. Was this the way it looked when I was inside? When he was raping me? Did he have someone in there now? Was someone else in danger?

The urge to run, but not being able. The urge to scream, but not being able. The feeling of going mad. It was too much. I turned my head away from the house and took a deep breath. I felt as if I was going to faint, and was afraid because he might find me out there in the bushes again. He might drag me into his house again . . .

I looked around, trying to stay sane. Families were playing behind me in the park, and an older couple was walking right in front of the house. I wanted to yell to everyone to stay away, to not be so close to something so evil. I wanted to protect everyone like I couldn't protect myself. I looked back at the house. The second floor had tasseled shades also, and I thought I saw the side of one move ever so slightly . . .

"Address! If you don't give it to me, I can't give you what you need!"

The man's sharp words brought me back to the present. I handed him the paper I'd pulled from my pocket. How long had I been standing there?

He came back about ten minutes later and handed me a huge, brown, leather-bound book. It had large numbers stamped in gold across the face, and it was too heavy to carry far. I took it to the nearest table and set it down. It was dusty and old and contained my answers. I didn't want to open it. But I did. I'd come too far. The fancy, cursive writing gave me the name and address of the owner.

Now I had someone to call. It took me a couple days, but I gathered my courage. I had to know. After looking in the library for phone numbers, I was ready.

"Hello?" she questioned again in a sing-song voice.

"I . . . I'd like to know if your grandson is available, please," I whispered, finding my voice. A second went by, maybe two. My heart pounded in my throat and ears. Had I guessed right? Was he her grandson, or her son? I had so little to go by. The information was vital to me.

"Which grandson, dear . . . Mark or Mike?" she asked. Mark. That was the name Rob had used in the hospital.

It was true. Rob had had me raped. His words burned into my mind: "I only wanted Mark to scare you . . . this is an added bonus." I had hoped and prayed that it wasn't true. The moment was astonishingly emotional for me.

"Mark . . . " I managed to whisper. I couldn't believe I might hear the voice of the man who'd raped me. I could never forget it, and I'd know right away if it was him. I would hang up as soon as he answered.

"I'm sorry, dear . . . Mark's no longer . . . with us. He died last year."

I couldn't believe what I was hearing. Anger. Frustration. More anger. Relief. I wouldn't have to hear his voice again. I was liberated from a terrible task, yet that feeling

quickly faded and was replaced with anger. How dare he die so that I can't confront him.
How dare he die and leave me with this pain.

"Were you a friend?" she continued.

"No, I . . . thank you for your time." Ever the polite girl. I hung up the phone. For
years, I tried to forget what he did to me. Even though he's dead, it's never ended for me.
I can't forget . . .

The despair I felt after my appointment with Gary hadn't let up, and it was
already Sunday. This was an unusually long time for me to feel such discourage-
ment. I wanted out. I wanted to quit. Even talking to Phil over dinner hadn't
allowed the feelings to dissipate.

Something deep, like a red-hot poker burning my flesh, stirred inside me
after the baby's birth. I wanted the rapist to suffer and be in pain. I wanted him
to cry out but for no one to come to his rescue. I wanted him to experience
isolation and loneliness and agony.

I obsessed about Rob. Why had he done this to me? Power? Did he fanta-
size about me in pain? About me dying? Did he want to know how it hurt me to
feel this man on top of me, inside me, the injuries, the pregnancy? The fear of
dying? Did he get off on the humiliating pain and isolation the man put me
through? Had they talked about me? Laughed about what they were going to
do? I dreaded going to sleep because I knew I would dream about the rape, and I
dreaded waking up because it had really happened.

I couldn't have men touch me or look at me because of the rape, and I knew
that Rob knew this. When I thought about him, emotions came into me like a
torrent of pain and memories. Everything I'd worked hard for, he took away. He
destroyed me. I was ashamed that when I thought of him, of that time, tears ran
down my cheeks. If I could have had everything that was done to me, done to
him, I would. I'd leave him broken in a thousand pieces.

That I had the ability to hate another person was surprising, and I had sudden misgivings about what I was doing. Therapy . . . all of it. Maybe I was
bringing out things in myself that were better left alone. Inside and hidden.

The memory of Rob's words in the hospital burned through me as I got
into the bath after our dinner. They broke through my pain for a moment that
day and destroyed my trust in everyone I knew. He had no idea of the pain he'd
caused me.

I made the water extra, extra hot and breathed as I lowered myself into it. As I picked up my journal, I realized I was moving into somewhere I wasn't at all sure I could, or should, go . . .

April 26, 1977

I'm scared that Rob's doing something to me. I woke up on the top bed of a twin bunk bed last night in a small, damp room in the basement of the hotel. I don't remember how I got there. The last thing I remember was talking to Bill upstairs in the conference room. I had no clothes on. I can't believe what's happened. I'm frightened that something's happening to me again. What have I done?

I was alone in the room and looking around for my clothes when the door opened and Rob and Mike walked in. Mike looked familiar, and Rob told me right away that he was Mark's brother. That's how he introduced him to me, as Mark's brother. Natural. Off-handed . . . but he kept looking at me in the eye, and he stood between me and the door.

I felt like I was going to be sick. How can he do this to me? How long can this go on? I became furious and started to speak, but he slapped me across the face. I'm afraid he's going to do something really bad to me.

He threw me my skirt and told me to get dressed. All I wanted to do was get out of there. I felt like someone had done something, but I didn't know what. It didn't feel like anyone had had intercourse with me, but just that they had been looking at me.

I want to go to the police. I have to do something about this. I can't handle it anymore, but . . . I know he's into something. His threats, even when I'm doing nothing, are awful. What will he do to me if I go to the police?

May 10, 1977

It's been several days since I've been able to write. The skin on my hands is so sore and scratched that I couldn't even hold a pen until now. The doctor bandaged it pretty tightly but said I wouldn't need stitches, and my side is killing me. I thought I was becoming a master at handling pain after the rape, but this has caught me off guard.

Rob came to my apartment a couple of days ago and took me back to the hotel. There was some kind of function he wanted me to go to because he had to work that evening, but I was afraid. I hadn't been to the hotel since I woke up with no clothes on. So I got hold of Rhonda and told her that I ended up in a bedroom downstairs and that I was afraid someone put something in my soda. She said we should watch out for each other. I'm so paranoid, I just want to get away from all these people, but I feel so trapped. It's going on forever, and I can't figure a way out. Rob will find me no matter where I go.

I didn't dare eat anything, and just had a couple of sips from a soda that I poured myself. I don't remember leaving it, but one minute I was okay, and the next moment my head was twirling around on my neck. I was so dizzy I couldn't stand, but I remember walking down a long alley, downstairs between the two buildings of the hotel. I was in a dream. As I walked, the alley just extended farther and farther away; it stretched on forever, and my feet didn't feel like they touched the earth. I'm not sure who was with me. The end of the alley seemed to move, to extend forever as we walked. I'm crying as I write this. I just want this fucking bad dream to be over.

I woke up later and, like before, I didn't have any clothes on, but this time I was on the lower bed of the bunk bed. I remember looking up at the springs and my head spinning and then closing my eyes and opening them again, trying to focus. I opened and closed my eyes several times. It took me a while, but my feet finally found the floor. I worked quickly to find my clothes and get dressed. I didn't want to see Rob or any of his friends.

As I picked up my shirt that was flung on a chair, I noticed a desk drawer that was open slightly. Inside, there were about fifty or sixty photographs of me. I couldn't believe my eyes. I was lying on a bed, naked. My eyes were open in some of them, but vacant and empty like I was dead. It was so frightening to see. So gruesome. I looked so defenseless and alone. It was like looking through someone else's eyes. I was horrified.

I grabbed the photos from the desk and wrapped them in my jacket. I was afraid I was going to run into somebody. I got dressed and ran out of the room. Back down along the alley. My legs were unsteady, and I was tearing the flesh on my hands on the concrete of the building.

I didn't see Rob or Mike or any of their friends. I ran and didn't look back. It was hard to ignore the pain in my side, and my breathing didn't return to normal once I reached the bottom of the hill.

I went straight to Dr. Monosh and told him I thought something was wrong with my lungs, but he told me after an x-ray that I had three broken ribs. When he asked me how it happened, I had to say that I didn't know. Humiliating.

Something gripped me around the throat, and I felt like I was going to throw up. I was so angry with Rob, with his friends. How could they do this to me? Rob has made my life miserable. Being with him is the worst mistake I've ever made, and I need to fix it.

May 12, 1977

I have to tell my mom the truth about everything that's happening. Even if it takes moving someplace where he won't find us, that's what I'll have to do. I'm afraid for my life. If something happens to me, perhaps they will find this and know where to look.

I threw my journal across the bathroom. I was so angry at Rob, at his control over me, at the control I'd *given* him over me. This had to stop. I resolved to talk to Gary about him at my next appointment, and end this hold he had over me.

I stood to wash the bath oil off me and used water so hot it nearly burned my skin. *I want all . . . this . . . gone.* And if it took burning the memories off me, I was going to do it.

Phil came into the bathroom to give me my towels when he heard me turn off the shower. Wrapping my towel tightly around me, he noticed my skin, bright red and nearly blistered. He just held me close without speaking.

Later, we drew the sheer curtains closed and lay on the bed, holding each other. Raindrops on the windows had made the lights beyond shine against the curtain like bright, cut diamonds. We made love. Again and again and again. A feeling of release and euphoria washed over me.

Chapter 13

July, 1996

"I'm ready to go back into the house, but I need you." I lowered my eyes as I said it. I still hated asking for Gary's help. I bit my lip, tasting salty blood.

"Is that what you'd like to work on today?" Gary asked.

"Yeah . . . I think it's important." Still, I didn't raise my eyes to look at him. I was afraid I'd start crying and I'd just started the session. I told him about the trip Phil and I took to San Francisco . . .

"Can we drive past it? Can we drive past where the house was again?" It was a tentative question. I wasn't sure how I wanted Phil to answer. I knew he'd do what I wanted, but I also trusted his instincts. Would it be a good idea to go past where that house used to be?

He stopped the car, turned toward me and took my hands in his. "Is that what you really want?"

"Yeah . . . I think it really is." We'd already checked into our hotel in San Francisco and were on our way to dinner. Going past where the house used to be would only take ten minutes or so. We were in town for Sally's graduation. I was so proud of her; she'd worked so hard.

We drove up Divisidero, up the hill flush with huge, stately Victorians, and turned the corner. It looked as it had nearly a year ago when we first drove past. We sat across the street from it and both of us became quiet. I looked past Phil, his silhouette framed in the car window, and thought back to the day that changed my life.

I understand suffering. I understand when someone says they hurt. When their heart is heavy. When they feel despair as if they have no purpose in life. I understand that.

I felt myself moving into a crevasse. Like I was sliding down a hill, but that there was were I needed to be. I needed to go down and then move back up. It's hard to explain.

I looked back at Gary. I was emotionally involved with him, something I'd really tried not to let happen; our relationship just seemed so intense and intimate. I know this is his job, but it's my life.

"I need to go back in the house, please . . . I need to go in to get out," I pleaded with him.

"Okay . . . relax, put your feet flat on the floor and close your eyes . . . " His voice grew warm and soft and comforting. I knew that I was safe. And I was back in the house relating what I saw, what I felt . . .

I'm standing there . . . looking at myself still. I'm on the mattress in front of me, and I'm just plastered to the wall on the opposite side of the room. I'm looking at myself. Just looking. I can't move, even though I want to more than anything. He's in back of me now, and he's . . . sodomizing me. I can't move to help myself. I need to help myself.

Last night I had a dream. A nightmare, really, but it began as a dream . . . a heavenly dream of dazzling, erotic, ethereal images. I was naked, sitting with my legs under me and my arms raised above me. I was in ecstasy. Spinning about my head were tiny lights like fireflies. Swirling about me, drawing me into a concentric circle. They were gentle with me at first, but became more and more frantic, more and more painful. My hair, falling below my waist, was lifted up . . . up . . . up. The swirling motion lifted me higher, straightening my back and then when it would stretch no further, it arched under the pressure.

I felt a tremendous pain in my tailbone. A chilling, stark pain that traveled up my spine inch by inch by inch. I arched more to relieve what was beyond pain by now. Each fraction of spine felt more intolerably painful than the last. Cramping spasms worked their way up to my neck and my head. Reflexively, I brought my head back until it touched my back. My hair felt heavy. My arms, still up, grasped in front of me for relief from the agony. For deliverance. Please, I screamed. Make the pain stop. My head and arms were forced down by heavy air. The intensity was painful yet orgasmic. The air

pushed my head down toward my chest and pressed my arms tight against my sides. It
swirled around my body, engulfing me like a cocoon. Pushing my pelvis deep into the
floor, I felt a sensation like birth. A movement through me that descended down along my
spine. A strand of DNA, golden . . . now silver . . . now golden again . . . dazzling and
brilliant . . . was engulfing me until a powerful orgasm brought it twisting around my
neck, strangling me . . .

My eyes popped open. I looked in Gary's eyes, then down at my hands in my
lap. Suddenly, being in the house had become about my sexuality. I felt trapped
and like I was choking. I brought my hand up to my throat and rubbed it, trying to
breathe easier. Though he was far too young, I came to think of Gary as a father. A
benevolent, caring father. One who, no matter my solicitation, wouldn't join me in
thinking less of me. *His children,* I thought, *are fortunate,* and I was forced to admit
an envy for them. He'd done what my own father couldn't.

Gary entered the house with me willingly and helped me to feel the plethora of
emotions that arose. He strove to understand the scared child I became in the
corner of the room when watching what unfolded in front of me. His concern for
me allowed me to close my eyes, imagine the scene, and know that he wouldn't
leave me in the house alone; he would not let me stay there without him.

One of Gary's priorities was to provide me with motivation to face the resistance and repression of which I'd become master. And when I told of feeling the
man's body on mine, of the choking sensations when remembering the cloth stuffed
in my mouth, of the smells in the stained mattress beneath me, and the sounds I
heard while imprisoned in my nightmare, he didn't turn away from me. Rather he
met my nightmare head-on, and gave me courage to do the same.

We combined his tenacity and my perseverance to form a powerful alliance
against the very defenses that previously protected me . . . defenses that out-
lived their usefulness and had to be understood and resolved. At first I brought
a clumsy, halting manner to our work as a team. Our commitment to a shared
goal, for me to become more truthful to myself, though, became more important than my discomfort and anxiety.

I wouldn't be seeing Gary for several weeks, and when I left his office, I was sad
that I didn't have more time to talk. My heart fell into this disturbing rhythm that
it had lately, and I couldn't figure it out. As if I was scared and didn't know how to
respond with my mind, and so was responding with my body.

We were leaving for Monterey that day, though, and like our trip to Bodega Bay, I thought maybe it was a good idea to take my journal from the next box. It was labeled *Sexuality*. Before opening it the previous day, I sat looking at it for several hours. I should have been eager to look inside and to read the journal, but I felt disconcerted somehow. I was reticent to upset the delicate balance that the contents held, and a remembrance of my disclaimer to my husband the first night we were intimate: "I've been raped." Nothing more.

We got to the hotel early in the afternoon. It was a European-style hotel, small but very intimate, right on the edge of the bay in Monterey. We were on the top floor with a panoramic view. A huge canopied feather bed with deep burgundy comforter invited us. A fireplace in the corner, a large armoire, a writing desk, two small settees in striped gold and burgundy, and an upholstered seat beneath the bay window made the room very warm and pleasant.

The bathroom was the same inviting color of soft burgundy in marble on the floors and the walls. A large Roman tub with a built-in shell-shaped pillow headrest tempted me. I thought about the *Sexuality* box I had looked in just before we left, and lit the cinnamon-laced candles along the side of the tub.

Inside were more photographs. Photographs I'd taken myself of the scars on my breasts, my hip, my legs, my hands. And in bold, angry strokes, a huge red "X" over them.

It was those photographs I remembered when I slipped into the bath, hot as boiling water, and picked up my journal.

June 14, 1977

I met a man last night while I was walking with Rob. His name is Phil. My life is going to change.

Today was the first time I've experienced my sexuality since the rape. It's the first time I've felt anything, when I looked at Phil. It was late when I got home. I looked in the mirror. All I saw were scars, but I kept looking and I saw his hands on my breasts, covering them with his big hands. I want to feel alive again. I want to exist again. And when I came home, I finally had an orgasm again for the first time since it happened. And all the while, I was thinking about Phil.

I closed the drapes and lay on my bed. I closed my eyes. Since the rape, all I've had when I closed my eyes are scenes of the man . . . but today I had scenes of Phil in my mind. I couldn't even see fantasies before, but today I saw Phil. I focused on the sensations my body was feeling. I was patient and sensitive with myself as I thought he might be. I touched my nipples, and they responded with the lightest touch.

I put my shirt back on. I can't stand to look at myself anymore, but I like looking through my blouse and seeing my nipple strain against the fabric.

My hand fell to my side and moved around my hips to the front. The feel of my hand along the soft skin of my abdomen felt pleasurable and sensual and comforting. Familiar. I feel some soreness from the surgery. My pain. Have I become so disconnected from it, from my body, that I don't feel anything at all until it's touched?

I became wet, though, and I let my finger rest inside me. I sank deeper into the mattress, feeling my body return to me. I had an image in my mind of Phil before me. He took a beautiful silver hairbrush from my night table. A shiver ran down my spine. The anticipation of him running the brush through my hair made my heart quicken. He moved behind me and placed the brush at the top of my head, brushing it against my back. My heavy breathing turned into small, low moans. I longed to reach behind me and touch him. He moved my hair to the front, covering my right breast and the scars from the rape. He didn't touch me for several seconds, but I could feel him near me. He gently pushed my head forward, touching my chin to my chest and caressing me lightly on the neck. His touch was lighter than I'd anticipated. I remained perfectly still. Like a small, delicate butterfly, his fingertips walked gently around the small of my back, up around my hips and along the curve of my stomach, and finally back to my shoulder. He didn't see the scar on my hip, or if he did, he didn't care. My desire for him was sweet and immediate.

June 17, 1977

It happened a year ago today.

I saw Phil again today, on the street outside the hotel. I was alone. He's so handsome. Tall, with a beautiful smile. His eyes smile too. When he spoke to me, I was so nervous I'm not even sure what I said.

I crave intimacy with a man. With this man. Just hold me and love me, just for one night, I want to say to him. But I can't imagine anyone wanting to be with me after what's happened. I waited so long, and that was ripped away. Now I'm uncomfortable showing him . . . well, I just can't imagine him seeing me with my scars.

I wish I was someone else.

July 2, 1977

Last night was like a dream! Phil came with Rob, Eddie, and Bill to pick me up from work. This job is fun, at least, a craft store where all I have to do is talk! Perfect.

As long as other people are around, I feel all right, but I'm still trying to get away from Rob. He's just in every nook and cranny of my life. I can't turn around, I can't make a move without him being right there.

Anyway, they brought Phil along. I couldn't believe my eyes! He's so handsome and tall. He was dressed in jeans and a white shirt. A long-sleeved, white shirt. It looked so good on him. He'd folded up the sleeves. He had a jean jacket on too, but had rolled up the sleeves of his jacket. His arms and his hands looked so strong. I wondered how it might feel to have him hold me.

The others went upstairs with John, but Phil stayed downstairs with me and listened to my little demonstration speech. He said he might be interested in buying a rug for his sister, which was sweet. I wonder if he even has a sister. It was just so nice of him to listen all the way through. No one's ever done that before.

Anyway, he helped me into the back seat of the Jeep, which was kind of him. My ribs still hurt, and it was difficult getting in and out. Rob sat on one side of me and Eddie on the other. Rob put his arm on the seat behind me, but I didn't want him close to me. Phil asked if we could stop at an ice cream place on Union Street before dropping me off, and everyone was okay with that. He got out of the Jeep and turned to us in the back, asking if anyone wanted anything. I didn't dare ask for anything. Rob had been hassling me more and more about my weight.

I watched as Phil walked into the ice cream parlor. His body was silhouetted against the neon frame of the doorway. I wanted to be out there with him. I wanted to be free. I was so afraid that I was going to cry. I wanted to be as far away from Rob and this Jeep as I could get. It was everything I could do to sit between them and not scramble for the door. For Phil.

He returned in a few minutes and opened the door. He looked in at me as if I was the only one in the Jeep, as if I was the only one in the whole world, and handed me a strawberry shake. "I thought you might enjoy this," he said with a huge, luscious smile.

I smiled back at him, an equally huge smile, happier than I'd been in a long, long time, smile. As I reached for the shake, my hand touched his ever so slightly. It was as if fireworks exploded in the car. I swear an electric current shot right through me! And he felt it too, I think. Time just seemed to stand still, and Phil's was the only face in the world for a moment. Just a moment, but it was long enough. Touching his hand took my breath away. I'll remember it always.

I thanked him and looked around. Had anyone else noticed what had just happened? Everyone was looking at Phil, but no one said a thing. No one said a thing.

July 22, 1977

Last night with Phil was pure magic. I can't believe what's happened. I feel as if I'm alive for the first time in a year. Even if I never see him again (I hope I see him again!), I'll never forget last night.

He saw me sitting on the steps, though I can't imagine why I was sitting on the steps, because I was on my way to meet Mom. But in any case, he saw me sitting there on the steps and asked where I was going. I told him, and he said he'd love to give me a ride. We got into his car and he said to me, "I'd like you to sit right next to me, close enough so that not even a piece of paper can pass between us." I'll never forget that.

He asked if he could take my mom and me to dinner at the Wharf, and of course (of course!) I said we'd love to go. Sitting at the table, his knee brushed against mine. Then lingered there a moment longer until he was certain of not having offended me.

When we returned to his apartment, we talked long into the evening about everything. Hopes, dreams. I wanted him to make love to me. The need to tell him of the rape, though, was pressing. I decided that if we were to become intimate, I needed to tell him about it.

His eyes grew soft and tender when I told him, and then he kissed me. It didn't stop him from wanting to make love to me.

I woke later that evening with my hand on his hip. We were facing each other, and I was afforded a moment to admire him. His body, his face is fresh and smooth and warm to my touch. His eyelashes are long and fine and look as if they're stretching to reach his eyebrows, they're so long. His breath was sweet and warm as it blew against my cheek.

July 30, 1977

Phil has saved my life. My sensuality since the rape is returning because of Phil's acceptance of me. Of my body. Of my experience. I deserve to be sexual, don't I? It's one of life's most luscious pleasures.

August 4, 1977

Rob came to Phil's door today, making a scene. He pounded on the door and told me to come out. He called me a whore and told me that he wasn't leaving without me. I was embarrassed beyond belief.

I turned to Phil. I didn't want him to see this. To see what kind of man Rob is, because I thought he'd think less of me. He looked in my eyes. Something in the way he looked at me told me not to be afraid ... that I'd never have to be afraid again. He put his hand on my shoulder and, without saying a word, moved me from in front of the door to around the corner in front of a closet.

He told me I had nothing to worry about, then he opened the door. I heard some words and looked out in time to see the back of Phil and the front of Rob, pressed against the wall. He put his head near Rob's ear and spoke softly, too softly for me to hear. Rob looked past Phil's shoulder into my eyes. I saw something I'd never seen before on Rob. Fear. He was afraid of Phil. It was glorious retribution. I can never thank Phil properly for what he's done.

It was late in the afternoon, and the Golden Gate Bridge was painted a bright orange by the setting sun. I'd not seen the view from Phil's apartment at that time of day, but I wanted to show him more. I wanted to show him all of me, with all my scars. I knew I would find acceptance in his eyes.

I laid out the blanket on the floor in the living room and slowly took off my skirt, then my nylons and panties. As he watched me, and our eyes locked in a sort of embrace, I took off my blouse.

He came over to me and kissed every inch of me, never flinching, never looking away. I felt so free when we made love. I've found acceptance.

August 17, 1977

I still haven't heard from or seen Rob. The thought that I might be free of him is too much to hope for, but . . . dare I even think it? I do. I will. I am. Free.

Chapter 14

September, 1996

"Desire, lust, sex . . . I never thought that the only reason we engage in intercourse is to procreate. I'm excited about what my body can do sexually."

It sounded defensive as I said it, as if I was trying to convince myself more than Gary. Fantasies became a safe, albeit lonely, way for me to experience my sexuality again after the rape. My body sent me messages, and it was my job to decipher those messages. My desire hadn't been destroyed, but I had to learn a new way to satisfy myself. A new way to accept my sexuality. My need for tenderness and compassion were all mixed up with disturbing, violent fantasies. Now those disturbing, violent fantasies were back.

No matter the effort, I had difficulty. At first the fantasy would be ethereal and lovely, then turn into a brutal cacophony of images. Of implements and sounds, particularly sounds. Screaming sounds. All the sounds I couldn't make during the rape filled my head. I wanted to put my past into a compartment that wouldn't touch my sexuality.

I was uncomfortable talking to Gary about this. We'd grown close and I felt anything but a prude . . . but, well, it was as if I was talking to my father about sex. My sexuality startled me and thrilled me . . . but mostly startleed me. The message: *Good Girls Don't* that I grew up with never fit. Ever. But the conflict between the message and the feelings brought shame. My body responded, and I was ashamed of that.

Sex is when I express myself most fully. I'm out of the prison of my mind and in the moment.

I wanted to tell Gary about the first time Phil and I made love . . .

His body was remarkable. There's nothing as arousing, as seductive, as a man who is confident in himself. Not boastful or egotistical, but assured. Strong and sure and confident of himself. Muscles just below the surface of his skin, ready to be called into action, but with a look of grace and poise, ready to fill me up with no room for anything, or anyone, else.

He was still asleep; I pushed against his shoulders and moved him onto his back. He woke with a stretch and a smile and pulled me close to him. Laughing, he brought me on top of him.

"Slowly," he said. "We have lots of time. Don't hurt yourself." He grasped my hips and eased me up. A moment of regret that I had opened myself up, ourselves up, to this must have passed across my face. Perhaps I shouldn't have told him about the rape. Perhaps I shouldn't have thought I was ready for this . . . perhaps it was still too fresh. It had been just short of a year since it happened. I had never made love with a man before; my only experience was excruciatingly painful, emotionally and physically. What made me think that all that was behind me? Would this hurt as the rape did?

It was as if he read my mind. He saw that I was afraid of disappointing him, disappointing myself. I didn't want to face the fact that my sexuality might have been compromised by what happened. He gave me a tender look and hugged me. I thought it was a sign that he was going to stop, but thankfully he did not.

He didn't move a muscle; we were as quiet as can be, just allowing me to feel him, to feel every emotion. I felt myself relaxing inside and moved toward him. The hunger for him, the desire for him to start moving, to move to a climax, made me flushed and anxious. I felt a sudden pulsating inside me, and the familiar tightening of an orgasm which was beyond reproach. His energy, his body, his flesh against mine urged me to release any pain and satisfy my longing and desire.

The days of pure indulgence in each other were an excess of pleasure and sensuality. There was no one else in our world. I talked to him like I couldn't with anyone else. He showed me passion and fire and gave me an appetite for pleasure and satisfaction.

Phil was never cognizant of the part he played in easing me into my sexuality. I never thought I'd feel this way, ever. And it has remained, steadfast and true. He can't know the part he played, or what it meant to me that my fantasies returned to a semblance of normalcy after we met; they had grown so violent and gruesome. Phil taught me the meaning of sexuality, of intimacy, and of love.

Chapter 15

October, 1996

"Never take the road to hell." He said it with clarity, yet that's how he said everything. With great clarity.

I'd been seeing Dennis as my internship supervisor for several months, and highly valued his opinion. While he had thirty-one years as a psychologist, and a great deal of technical knowledge, he also had keen insight to people and their motivations and a rare combination of empathy and logic.

We rarely stepped outside our professional relationship, but not because of a wall he'd erected, so today I told him about a conversation I'd had with one of my other program advisors. I felt it fell under the auspices of what we were working on . . . sort of . . .

"Well . . . I have something I want to mention to you, Teresa. I'd be remiss if I didn't."

Dick's words brought me around. I could barely see his face, the sun was so blinding. He'd wanted to meet outside at a cafe around the corner from his office. It was near a large university and was suitably trendy with its mix of professors and students. After a year as my advisor for my graduate program, it was time to terminate. This was our final meeting.

I tried to focus on his face, but I was seeing double. My cold had become serious in the last couple of weeks, and it was all I could do to get up in the morning. But I was close to the end of my program and intent on finishing my requirements: two last major papers, completing my intern hours, and terminating with my advisor. Today. This couldn't wait, not even for the fever that started this morning. It was excruciatingly hot sitting there in the sun, even though the air was chilly.

He'd rolled up the sleeves of his crisp, white shirt. It was the first time I'd even seen him without his jacket on. He was a small, slight man with light gray eyes behind round, black glasses. He dressed impeccably, and liked to talk about himself in the third person. Interesting. It always gave me the creeps when he did that.

"You want to be a sex therapist. Do you like to do it?"

"What?" I thought it must have been the fever. He couldn't have said what I thought he said.

"Do you . . . like to do it?" Yeah, he'd said what I thought he'd said, and repeated it. "Well, I'll tell you . . . " he went on ". . . since you do, you'll be way ahead of the rest. I think you're going to have difficulty becoming very successful as a sex therapist, though, at the weight you're at. No one's going to take you seriously."

"What?" I was making more and more sense, I'm sure.

"You're very pretty. You have a very pretty face. And you're sharp, I can see that. I can sense these things about people. But no one's going to take you seriously at the weight you're at. They're going to think you're out of control."

I sat there in disbelief at what this man was saying to me. My grades (excellent) didn't matter. My relationship with my clients (excellent) didn't matter. My history (certainly suited to understanding others' suffering) didn't matter. My empathy, my compassion, my intelligence, my personality. None of it mattered because my hips weren't thirty-six inches around. Had this been on his mind as he guided me through difficult cases? Had this been an issue as he accepted my money for his services for the past year?

I was furious. I couldn't believe he was sitting in judgment of me, of my physical body as an indicator of how I'd do my job. My face was aching and sore and I was unbearably hot, and I just didn't know what to say. I didn't know how to respond. Tears were welling up in my eyes and at risk of spilling over onto my cheeks. I didn't want to cry in front of him, to let him see how much he'd hurt me, so I turned away and mumbled something inane. I believe I thanked him for his time. Thanked him for his time! By the time I left, I was more angry at myself for letting him off the hook.

How could he understand? How could anybody? I'd hidden my body under a suit of armor. I needed it. I needed to feel safe and like no one was ever going to hurt me again. I needed to keep people away. And if someone did try to hurt me, at least they couldn't have hurt me as badly as the man who raped me. I remember flying through the air in his house. I didn't want to fly through air again.

"Well, I have two other policies *I* live by that might help," Dennis said after I finished the whole story. "I never do anything to hurt myself, and I never allow others to hurt me."

And he'd identified the root of my problem; that was what I had been doing. His words were so simple, so eloquent, yet so powerful . . . if I could integrate new behaviors into my existing situations.

The betrayal didn't stop with Rob. I betrayed myself after the rape. I remember the nineteen-year-old girl staring back at me in the mirror. It was the Monday before the rape, and I'd reached my goal of losing one hundred pounds. One hundred pounds . . . amazing. An entire person. It was my most significant accomplishment to that point. I'd bought the dress I was wearing ten months before, during the previous summer. It had an empire waist and was yellow and white with white piping at the edge of a soft, round neckline. My hair, always long and dark, framed a smaller face than I'd ever seen looking back at me. I never felt as pretty as I did the day I looked in the mirror. Pretty and something I'd never been called . . . petite.

As soon as I got home from the meeting with Dick, I ran to the box marked *Betrayal.* It occurred to me that I went through life unaware of the effect I have on others, but painfully aware of their effect on me. For each Dick that I'd met, for each time I hadn't spoken my mind and told them they were out of line to comment on my body, I'd betrayed myself. I'd become an accomplice with them in harming myself.

I ripped open the box. We were in the midst of packing. I really didn't have time to go into the boxes again, but there was a journal inside. As always, I'd kept a journal. The first entry was one I'd completely forgotten about writing, three days before the rape . . .

June 14, 1976

I've been so anonymous my whole life. Not any more! Guys are looking at me now. I can't believe the difference between fat and thin. It's like a secret society somewhere that I never knew existed. I can't imagine that everyone who is thin gets this much attention. It must become second nature to thin girls who get looks all the time, and attention.

I felt so see-through. After nineteen years, I'm finally free. A man held the door for me yesterday while I was downtown shopping. I didn't know how good this would feel, for a man to hold the door open for me. Such tremendous effort, but it's over now. Two years of the most intense work I've ever done.

Rob's getting more and more strange about it, though. I thought he'd be happy for me. He knows better than anyone how hard this is. I thought he'd be proud of me, but he always seems angry, or annoyed. I know he's working a lot, but he seems so angry at me. He asked me the other day if I thought Bill was cute, and I said he was okay, but I noticed him looking at me while I was talking to him. I asked Rob if anything was wrong, but he just walked away. I'm only nice to his friends because they're his friends.

I feel my sexuality is heightened. I wonder what's going to happen next!

I had to take a moment before continuing; it was hard to keep reading through my tears. It was hard to believe what happened next, hard to believe that I had been so naive and innocent. The other entries in the journal in the *Betrayal* box were after I'd met Phil . . .

July 20, 1977

It's been over a year since the rape, and I've gained almost all the weight back. Too much time went by, seven and a half months, between the rape and learning it was Rob. I thought I'd sabotaged myself by losing weight. I thought I'd sent out signals I was unaware of. My new body betrayed me. I thought if I hadn't lost weight, perhaps he wouldn't have noticed me. He wouldn't have been able to overpower me. My mind reasoned that I hadn't been raped when I was fat. Thin = rape. Fat = no rape. It all seemed so clear-cut to me. And so, the armor has gone back on.

All the work I'd done trying to feel as if I was worth losing the weight. The rape has been the death of me. And my lifelong obsession with food is back. There's comfort in food, I guess. In the act of eating. For a year, I've felt like I needed to throw up. Eating is the only thing that makes that go away. Eating is under MY control. Not anyone else's. I decide what I want to eat and when I want to eat it. It's intimate.

Now I've added another problem to my eating. Now I feel like I'm stroking myself with the food. As if I'm saying to myself that because I've been through the rape and all the shit, I deserve to eat what I want. I'm in a circle. There's no motivation behind my cravings. No long-term satisfaction. All I feel is a black hole in my stomach. Food. Gimme.

I just feel tremendous grief and sorrow for what I've done to my body.

July 22, 1977

I read and read and read and still I've found no answers about why men rape. Some men. Few men. Probably a minuscule number of men. And what's happened inside me that I've put all my weight back on? Why do I feel such shame? Now I feel shame about gaining weight. Shame on top of shame. Shit. Meeting Phil has been wonderful, but I wish he'd met me while I was thin.

I laid the journal down on the table. It was the last entry for a while. I'd been reading everything I could get my hands on since seeing Gary, and still found no answers on how to solve my problem. On how to feel comfortable inside my own skin. On how to take off my suit of armor and feel safe.

My weight gain can't be from lack of willpower, I thought. *I have more than enough willpower. More than enough motivation regarding other things in my life.* And I did. A successful marriage, a successful business, but yet, the ability to control my weight was elusive. And I found no answers, so I read more.

That many women feel shame following rape is a fact. That rape is a power issue and not a sexual one is a fact. But facts meant nothing to me without being able to apply them to myself personally. So I started reading about rapists. Maybe there was a clue as to what kind of person he was and how the intersecting of our lives affected me and my relationship to my body.

There are, I learned, four different "kinds" of rapists. Mine (mine?) had been a "sadistic" rapist. *Aren't they all?* the thought occurred to me, but I read on. Sadistic rapists use implements like cigarettes, sticks, bottles, whips, electrical shock devices, and they aren't satisfied with just inflicting pain. Strangulation and mutilation are most often committed by the sadistic rapist. They tend to direct their violence at body parts with sexual significance: breasts, buttocks, mouth, anus, and genitalia.

The research was there: manners of rape, methods, some information — but not enough — on motivation. True motivation.

But precious little about why I responded the way I did after being raped. Little about why I had felt the need to change my body in order to feel safe. Little about how I could integrate such a painfully intrusive experience into my sexual life, into my everyday life.

All the journals had been difficult to read, and all of the boxes had been hard to open and look at. But this one, the one I'd marked *Betrayal,* was especially so.

It was the fall-out, the consequences of what had happened. It was what happened after people read the story in the newspaper. It was the result of what those fourteen hours did to me.

My lack of confidence and self-worth was so evident in my journal, and I was angry, not so much at myself this time, but at the fact that I'd bought the program. I'd accepted the fact that I wasn't worthy unless I was thin. That my body size was tied to my worth as a human being. I was in the midst of redefining myself, though I hadn't realized it at that point.

And people like Dick just facilitated my willingness to keep betraying myself. The choice was mine, as Dennis said. I could *choose* to take the road to hell, I could *choose* to hurt myself, I could *choose* to allow other others to hurt me. More importantly though, he went on to explain that I might simply be on auto-pilot and was in fact not realizing that I even had a choice. For if I did, why would I have kept choosing to harm myself? What was the payoff, the reward in that? His words were simple, yet profound and gave me much to think about.

Dennis's final words before I left came back to me . . .

"You know, Teresa, the truth really will set you free." So simple. So profound.

Chapter 16

January, 1997

"You're standing on a high diving board," Gary said. "Alone. Phil and I can watch you from the sides. We can cheer you on, but you're up there alone."

He was right, but I couldn't seem to stand up there for long by myself. Gary would say something in a certain way, show me compassion, and I would become quiet and retreat. That seemed to be my favored position. Retreat. I was embarrassed by his compassion, as if needing it made me appear weak and emotional. I could never ask for it. I remember reaching out for the nurse when I was in labor. I remember begging the man through a broken jaw to please not hurt me anymore. I remember wanting the man who asked if I was okay to get me some help.

I looked around his office. I felt so comfortable and safe here, and I liked the smell; it was familiar, for some reason, and I'd come to associate it with him. It was an inside office and dark, with two lamps for light. He had a desk the color of deep brown chocolate that he told me his father had built for him. I could see by the way he said it that it meant a great deal to him, and I was flattered that he'd shared a small piece of himself with me.

I knew that his function as my psychologist was not to share his life with me, and as a rule, he didn't. But this small glimpse into *him* allowed me to see him more as a person with the same feelings and desires and problems as anyone. Of course, on a thinking level, I knew that was the case, but I became wrapped up in my own thoughts and feelings, as his office was the only place where I allowed myself to do so.

Words became my comfort. Written, spoken, they were all opportunities for intimacy, if only for a moment. But particularly, words other people so kindly said to me. My own words to myself were even slowly beginning to comfort. Ever so slowly.

Each of us *are* alone in our experiences. We can empathize, we can develop compassion for each other, but we can't live each others' lives. We can't know how another person truly feels without sharing our feelings with each other. And I deeply needed that intimacy with others, if only for a moment.

I'd had just one of those moments that I wanted to relate to Gary . . .

The waiting room was small, and I'd read the chart on the wall several times before Dr. Hammond walked in. The pain in my jaw was still interfering with my life. The two surgeries I'd had to realign it had made a difference, but only temporarily. And the headaches were awful. They made me difficult for me to live with sometimes.

He had a kind face and a gentle, sweet manner. But his eyes truly showed his compassion. He was extremely easy to talk to. When he asked how I'd injured my jaw, he didn't hurry me along, but let me ramble and stammer and finally get to the point. And when he came to the question that I dreaded, that everyone had asked so far, whether I'd tried any type of mechanical device to alleviate the pain, I told him I couldn't use anything like that because the rapist had tried to have oral sex with me and then had stuffed a cloth in my mouth. His manner, his acceptance of me allowed me to express myself to him. He suggested a Body Awareness Class which had been enormously successful in helping patients with chronic pain.

I'd placed a great deal of hope in Dr. Hammond's class, and came motivated to change the relationship I had with my body. The class was held in a first-floor room with huge floor-to-ceiling windows that looked out over a pond. Even though there was a soft rain falling, there were still lots of ducks of all varieties playing and splashing. Being January, the sky was getting dark early, but the weather was so rainy and overcast that it made it seem later than it was.

During the first session, everyone introduced themselves and stated what had brought them to the class. While I never wanted anyone to have experienced rape, of course, I continued to look for a connection with someone who would understand. I declined to talk the first night, but decided that I would talk the following week. Everyone seemed so open and honest about their own struggles. They were all, every one of them, incredibly courageous.

As we moved into the floor exercises, I longed for Dr. Hammond's voice moving over me to calm my breathing and to make what was coming next not come. But it did.

We were on the floor, on our backs, practicing relaxation. Dr. Hammond's voice softly instructed us to release . . . close our eyes . . . feel our abdomen rise as we breathed in and fall as we exhaled. To pay attention to the rhythm of our bodies. His soothing words and encouragement of relaxation moved slowly from our feet to our calves to our thighs.

My breathing became more erratic and I squirmed, feeling cramps begin in my back as they had during the rape, and as they had returned since being in therapy. He moved his attention to our chest, arms, necks . . . when suddenly I felt the rapist on top of me.

"Please . . . not here . . . " I pleaded with myself to hold on to the present. I was trapped in a strange place. My body reacted as if I were on the mattress being raped, but my mind was active and keen. I was acutely aware of what was happening to me, not like other flashbacks in which I had little concept of where I was for minutes at a time. I struggled not to descend fully into the flashback.

It was the first time I experienced a sensation in which I felt I had a tiny bit of choice. That I could, if I expended a great deal of effort, gain control over it. I smelled smells, heard sounds, saw images, but dared not move in order to allow the soft haze of having choice move gently away from me. The intense cramps in my back kept my efforts focused on Dr. Hammond's voice. My back arched from the cramps, they were so intense.

As everyone was putting away their mats, Dr. Hammond came over to me and asked what had happened. He said I looked as if I was in distress. I was, I responded, but I told him I was willing to try again, and again, and again, if that's what it took. I was touched by his compassion for me, that he'd noticed the difficulty I was having. If only I could give that compassion to myself.

"Are you going to continue the class?" Gary asked.

"No. The flashbacks are just getting worse when I lie on the floor doing the exercises. But that first one . . . that makes me think I can get control over them, don't you think?" I looked at Gary as if he had all the answers. There was a part of me that believed he did, and that he was doing his job in making me work for the answers on my own. And I liked that he asked what I was going to do. It was such a minor thing, really, but he was teaching me to do what was right for *me*.

The thought flashed through my mind that I wouldn't have him to guide me much longer; that I'd have to start finding my own way. We'd talked the previous week about termination.

Termination. I knew it was coming. I'd been seeing Gary for two years, and it was time. Still, I felt lost when I thought of not having him to help me interpret the intense feelings I was still having. I would, he told me, have to start to determine my own course. To determine what I still needed from therapy. It was time for me to be in charge. And so, I made a list of the symptoms I was still having and prioritized their importance.

Chapter 17

March, 1997

We reached a bend in the road and found a bench. Seals barking and tripping over each other in search of the perfect warm rock, ducks bobbing butt-up, fishing for their supper, and the most beautifully moody clouds moved across the horizon. So breathtaking. My hair whipped against my face as we walked, the wind was so fierce. Phil draped his arm over my shoulder to keep me steady. That he wanted to talk wasn't altogether unexpected. He'd always been the one to believe that communication was vital to our relationship. The past several years had been disruptive, to say the least.

"You can cry . . . go ahead." Phil kept his arms around me. I needed the compassion and love only he could provide, but had the most difficult time giving him the opportunity. I just didn't, couldn't, open my heart and let him in, but not telling finally became far more painful than telling. It's so rare when things make sense, when the fog clears and things become focused and clear. I felt the opportunity for us to reach a new level of intimacy. The fact that we talked as much as we did was a measure of progress.

"Dr. Wright was interviewing my mom when we went to see him today." I just started talking, with no real idea where this would lead. "When she said she didn't have any grandchildren, he turned to me and said, 'Why not?' I know he didn't say it to be mean, and I know he didn't want an answer, but . . . it just hurts so much."

I put my head in his chest. His breathing never changed. He was as strong and sure and steady after, as he had been before, something I admired and counted on. He didn't say anything. He didn't try to make it better; he just let me cry. It was as if we both realized at the same moment that things just *are* sometimes. It didn't mean that I shouldn't express my feelings, and it didn't mean that he should try to "fix" whatever it was. It was just a fact that there was a hole in my heart where my child was. It was just a fact that I wouldn't have any biological children.

I pulled out a note that I'd written to him many years ago when he was out of town on my birthday . . .

February 12, 1982

A thought that is never far from my mind (even after all these years) is the child I had before we met. I still have so much sadness and guilt surrounding what happened that my heart never let go. I feel as if I let God down. Everyone says that time heals all wounds and I guess it does, but I remember those several days as if it were yesterday. I can remember the man on top of me and punching me when he was done. He just kept hitting me and hitting me all over. Harder with each punch rather than lighter, like you'd expect when someone gets tired. I kept thinking to myself (like when you feel you can't take one more second of something), "Just hold on . . . it will be over . . . one way or another . . . in a minute." It was, and I never thought I'd have to think about him again. And then the baby . . . how could God leave me there like that?

Such simple-mindedness. Suddenly it irritated me. Why had my intellect failed me when I needed it most? The facts moved through my head like a freight train. I was raped. I became pregnant from the rape. The baby was in serious trouble and my doctor felt that in order to give me the best chance of survival, he had to terminate the pregnancy when he did. Those were the facts.

"I have to tell her, you know. I have to tell my mom what happened." It was more to convince myself than to convince Phil. Each time she mentioned Rob or the baby, my heart broke a little more inside. I just wasn't able to share myself with her, and I hated it. I was forty years old . . . old enough to not need my mom's approval any longer. I had done the best I could for my situation.

"Yes. You should. Plan how you'd like to do it, and do it on your own terms, in your own time." I was surprised at Phil's response. He responded as if he had thought about it previously and already knew how he would respond.

Because of all the work I'd done, tears came easily, for which I was glad. Instead of feeling that they were a sign of weakness, I was slowly realizing my tears were simply a way that I best expressed my emotions. And those emotions were so strong. I constantly appraised myself in order to determine when Phil might tire of them and become anxious to move on.

I looked at him for a moment through my tears. He'd shown me in so many ways, over so many years, that my expectations had nothing to do with our reality. His deep brown eyes that I fell in love with the moment we met held such compassion for me. Such concern. My mouth opened to speak, but nothing came out. I was desperate to share my soul with him. Honesty and intimacy with him has always been an ideal to which I aspired. I knew I had to venture further outside my comfort zone in order to help Phil understand me.

We'd had difficult times. Many of them. On the outside, I looked so perfectly normal, but right under the surface were emotions that scared me to death. I'd been on my own for many years during our relationship, due to our business and his having to be away, and so many things had happened. But I had to be self-reliant. I had to take care of myself.

I wanted to tell him, particularly when we had a fight, how much pain I was in. I'd rush from the room, aching for him to follow me, to pry my feelings from me. I wanted him to know it wasn't for dramatics or because I wasn't being moody or sullen, I just hurt inside. I wanted to tell him all that was in my blood, my skin, my bones. What I hadn't realized was that my behavior was the very thing keeping us apart.

I was angry. Angry for all the time I'd spent feeling guilt and shame and remorse. Angry for decisions that were made *for* me. Angry that I'd turned the anger inside me instead of outside me where it belonged.

I found I could no longer believe without question.

My desecrated, raped self-worth had enabled me to accept the unacceptable. To feel as if I didn't matter.

It had kept me from asking for help when the man stopped me outside the house that day. It had kept me from going to the police. It had kept me from telling the people closest to me. It had kept me in my own private hell.

Chapter 18

June, 1997

"You don't respond when I use the word 'victim,'" Gary said, trying to look in my eyes. I kept them lowered. His statement was firm and adamant, designed to let me know this was something he thought was important.

"No . . . I don't like the word. I'm not. I'm just a . . . "

"You were just a pretty young girl taken advantage of by people you trusted. You were a victim."

Simple, clean, I thought. *His words don't leave me any room for guilt or shame on my part, so why do I still feel so bad? Why isn't this over?*

So I put the word "victim" off to the side; it was weakness and implied that I needed him, and I didn't want that. I didn't like getting attached, yet I realized that's just what had happened with Gary. It was completely contrary to what I felt I needed, but his tenderness and compassion with my feelings got the better of me. I hated the hungry, wanting part of me, but even that familiar feeling was becoming unacceptable and annoying. I just didn't want to hate anything about myself any longer.

"Well . . . I don't know. I'll have to think about it," I replied. It had become my motto when I was confused and unable to sort out the feelings at that particular moment. While it might have sounded like a brush-off, I didn't mean for it to. I really *did* think about everything we talked about each week. Everything.

I changed the subject. I wanted to talk about something light and fun and something I thought was unrelated to anything we'd been working on. I just didn't want to *feel* that day. He knew I had been in Sally's wedding the previous Saturday, so I found myself talking about the day of the wedding . . .

Sally treated us to an entire day at the spa, the day of the wedding. It was beautiful, decorated in a Roman motif with muted apricot and soft gray colors. Soothing. And I needed to relax. I'd never been in a wedding, and I was scared to death that I'd mess up the lines that Sally had entrusted to me. During frantic last-minute preparations over the past several days, I'd gone over and over the lines. Needless to say, I was nervous.

Each of us — there were four of us in the wedding party — went into separate rooms. Tracie, my masseuse, led me upstairs to a private area in the building. She was young and had beautiful skin and long, straight black hair. She opened the door to the room we'd be using. It was even more beautiful than the other areas. It was decorated in the same muted apricots and grays and had two huge columns not far inside the door, between which was draped a soft apricot sheer drapery. A beautiful ivy coiled its way up one column across the drapery and halfway down the other. Between the two columns hung a painting of a woman, Rubinesque, languishing in a Roman spa.

In front of the columns were two overstuffed, oyster-colored chairs. She invited me to take off my clothes and put on a fluffy terrycloth robe and slippers. She brought me coffee before disappearing around the drapery to get ready. I heard her turning on machines and then the stereo. Soft, sweet music filled the area. When she came back, she'd taken off her street clothes, had a smock on, and wasn't wearing shoes.

She led me back to one of the massage tables. First, she explained, she'd be doing a hot wrap. In getting ready, she'd give me a rub-down, then spread hot oil all over me, then wrap me in a warm foil. While she was doing that, she'd give me a facial. Then, after that was all over, a massage. It all sounded wonderful.

First she had me lie on my stomach. Her hands were soft and sensuous as they made their way up my legs, up my thighs, my hips, my back, shoulders, arms, hands. When she was finished, she asked that I turn over and started the same motion. Up my legs, my thighs, my abdomen. I mentioned that I was going to start my period and that it felt like the massage would be perfect for releasing tension in those muscles. She told me that she had many women who wanted her to concentrate on their legs, thighs, and abdomen when they were having their periods or right before.

Her hands moved to my hip bones. Her fingers on both hands at the same time made small circular motions over the bones and down into my abdomen. She said that I seemed tense in my abdominal muscles, and pressed harder into the area. She moved over to my left hip bone and worked again, rubbing, soothing, massaging up higher, then over; one hand over the other, she worked her way to the other side and then deep into the abdominal muscle once again. I felt the cramps subside ever so softly, like tiny ripples on the water.

Tears came to my eyes. I was as surprised as she was, and she asked me what was wrong. I told her nothing was wrong, that I was emotional because of the wedding . . . but what I was thinking about was the baby. About having someone with me at the time of her birth. About having someone's hands on me and how I had longed for someone to touch me like she was touching me now.

"You have to let your baby die. You're keeping her alive." Gary's words brought me back into his office, back into the present. Tears were streaming down my face. I hadn't realized how hard I'd been crying. I'd thought about her, in some form or fashion, nearly every day since it had happened. I'd allowed myself to continue to be raped, to continue to be in labor with the baby. *I'd* allowed it. I just didn't know how to stop it.

I'd held her inside me for twenty years, and it was time to let her go. But how? My body wanted to finish the job it started. I'd felt her come out of me, but couldn't hold her or put her lips to my breast. I held her inside me for a reason. What choice did I have?

My dependence on Gary was unsettling. His approval of me was too significant. I continued to remind myself that he wasn't my father, or a personal friend, but a professional here to help me help myself. The line that distinguished me from someone else sometimes felt blurred. I don't seem to recognize where I end and they begin, and I start feeling chaotic inside. *And besides,* I tried my best to reason, *if I have a problem becoming attached to people, growing close to them because I dread their leaving me . . . well, what's to be gained by becoming attached to him? After all, one of the goals of our relationship is for him to leave me.*

I couldn't figure out the answer. It was a catch-22. I'd tried not to become intimate with Gary, feeling that it would be more difficult when I left therapy, yet intimacy was the very issue I had to work on. It became evident that it was crucial in order to be able to confide in him.

Chapter

September, 1997

"The blood. It was all over the place. It was awful." I started shaking again as I remembered the thick, red blood running down Phil's face and covering his hand as he pressed it against the cut on his head. I had been anxious to see Gary.

"What happened?" Gary looked concerned, and his eyes grew more intense. I hadn't meant for it to sound as dramatic as it had come out.

"He was bending over fixing a speaker when he brought his head up real fast and banged it against the corner of the fireplace mantle."

"He's okay?" Gary asked. I liked that he was concerned about Phil.

"He's fine now. He had a headache for a few days, but ... "

Gary leaned back in his chair. He could see that Phil's injury, although I'd been very worried about him, wasn't the reason I'd brought this up, but rather a catalyst to something else. "Keep going ... "

His encouragement was appreciated, and it helped me tell him the whole story ...

It was late by the time we stopped working, and we were looking forward to relaxing and watching a movie. I sat reading until Phil got done setting up the speakers. We'd moved into our new home months before, but he knew if the speakers were even slightly maladjusted. So I picked up a magazine, knowing it would take him a couple of minutes.

I heard a sickening thud and looked up to see Phil looking at me with his hand on his head. Already, blood had flowed down his face like tributaries flowing from one major river. He looked confused at what he'd done and that blood was flowing so quickly.

We both snapped into action at the same moment. He ran toward the bathroom, blood streaming from his head through his hands. When I made it to the bathroom a millisecond after him, he'd already bent his head over into the sink and was applying pressure with a towel. It was nearly soaked through already.

I must have asked if he needed an ambulance or if he wanted me to take him to the hospital, because I remember him saying no . . . that he thought the bleeding was letting up a little. I looked down in the sink, and there was another bloody towel; he was already on the second. He pulled the towel off his head for a moment to look at it, and it did look as if the bleeding had let up a bit. And then he looked at me.

I felt as if I was being pulled farther and farther back, like I was in a tunnel. The look of the blood on his face, his tee shirt, and even on his shorts. The stunned look in his eyes. The smell of blood. I needed to be there with him . . . I needed to help him . . . but I could feel myself being pulled into a flashback. Into a horrible, fucking flashback. The smell of blood was the trigger.

This time was different, though. I'm not sure why. Whether it was because Phil needed me, or whether the therapy was making a difference, but I didn't go back. Not all the way, anyway. The images in front of me were opaque, transparent almost. But there nonetheless.

I saw myself standing in my home after the rape, looking in the mirror. This was something I hadn't remembered up to that point. It was something I hadn't wanted to remember. For the first time, I was able to see myself as I looked that day. I was able to see the way I looked to the man on the street who asked me if I was all right. And for the first time, I remember thinking that what happened to me was wrong, really wrong, and that the man should have helped me. Someone should have helped me.

I saw myself standing in front of the mirror. I remember taking an inventory. My hair was tangled, matted around my face. My forehead had a couple of cuts, but nothing too bad. My right eye was swollen but not shut, probably from my jaw; I didn't think he'd hit me in the eye.

The right side of my face was horribly swollen. My chin was slightly to the left. My lips were parted and cut, and my teeth were red. My mouth was filled with blood. Some of it had dried onto my teeth and lips, but some was bright red and moist. I moved my lower lip and felt my teeth move along with it. I remember putting my hand up to my mouth and noticing cuts on the outside of my hand. I moved my tongue back and my lip forward. My teeth, four of them in the front, held on by their roots.

I looked at my eyes in the mirror. I remember thinking that I was so young. This couldn't have happened to me. I must be in a dream. I looked farther down. I had my coat over me, but just barely, and a shirt under that but it was unbuttoned. My skirt, a jean skirt with snaps down the front, was only barely on also, and the snaps I'd managed to fasten were mismatched. All down the front of me, where my shirt and coat didn't cover, my chest was covered in blood. Most old and dried, but some, along the right side of my chest and shoulder, was new, red blood. I touched it with my finger, and it was still warm and wet.

"How could that man let me go? How could he look in my eyes and see how badly I was hurt, and let me go?" I was breathing heavily when I got through with the story.

Silence. Respectful again, of course, but silence nonetheless. It's not that Gary didn't want to tell me the answer; it's that there was none. There was no answer for why the man didn't help me. There was no answer for any of what had happened. I'd driven myself crazy looking for answers in the past, with only a nagging, restless feeling that I deserved it all. But that couldn't be the answer. It couldn't.

"I told my mom. Well . . . actually, I gave her the manuscript to read."

Gary looked surprised. "How did she take it?"

"She took it really well. We talked like we've never been able to. Just the two of us went out together for breakfast, and we talked and got all teary. She asked if it was all right if she could ask me questions every now and then, and I said, sure."

"I'm proud of you. I know how difficult it was for you to do this," Gary said.

As I sat in his office, I felt grateful that I had him to share this with. He'd done so much to help me find my voice; I was finally able to speak because of him. I knew he would encourage me to tell Phil about what had happened to me the night I had the flashback, and that I would be glad that I did.

Chapter

October, 1997

My greatest learning, my greatest insight, occurs when I least expect it . . . when I'm most afraid, when I'm most discouraged. And so it was with this most recent realization, simple yet profound. My guilt had served a purpose. I needed it, because if I felt guilt, then it meant that I had control over everything that had happened. If I had no control, then my life didn't make sense.

While packing to go to my dad's funeral, I threw a blank journal book into my suitcase. It saved my sanity. The envelope sat before me now. I'd never read it, not even after I wrote it originally. It contained the raw emotions of a young girl two days after a brutal rape. It wasn't pretty, but it was my truth. My nineteen-year-old handwriting, shouting out a warning to anyone who comes close, couldn't haunt me any longer if I faced it. It couldn't make my skin hurt and my bones ache if I faced it. And so I looked inside . . .

June 21, 1976

I feel as if I'm in a dream, or a sick joke. This can't be happening to me. What have I done? How could something so horrendous happen? I can barely write this . . . putting in words . . . seeing them before me is so surreal. Yet keeping it inside me is not an option. I feel so old. My dignity is gone. People are staring at me as if I'm a freak. I know they know.

Taking the train might have been a huge mistake. Money. Always money. I'm so tired of living with less. Working harder . . . living with less. Only $150 more, and I would have had airfare. As it is, everything I've saved is gone. Too late now. I'm terribly uncomfortable. My hip, my jaw, my hands, my breasts, everything hurts. I can't eat.

I'll never be able to forget that man's face. His eyes. I don't understand any of this. Why me? It really was a mistake to take the train. Everyone knows. God, please . . . please . . . please make this just be a bad dream. Make it all go away. I can't sit still. I have to walk around. I have to get out of here. I'm jumping out of my skin. Please stop the train! Please let me off! I have to get out of here!

I had to stop writing. I feel as if I'm going crazy. I walked back and forth in the car I'm in for the longest time. People are looking at me like I'm crazy, but I just can't sit still. Like I'm trapped here. It's getting darker outside, and this constant rumble, rumble back and forth . . . I just want to be off this train. I'm so hungry. Dr. Johnson said it will be six weeks before I can eat good again. I'm so hungry. Maybe a milkshake or something would be good. I can't do this alone. I keep tearing up. I'm so afraid to start crying . . . I won't be able to stop. Even the tears hurt my skin, everything feels so sensitive, so sore. Why me? Why did this happen to me? So why not me? What makes me so fucking special? It's obvious. Nothing.

Most people are sleeping now. So much time has passed since I wrote the last sentence. My mind is turning over and over. I'm so confused. I can't stand this feeling. All I feel is him inside me. His hands on top of me. Inside me. I waited so long. I'm sorry now for waiting; it would have been better for me not to have waited. I'm nineteen, for God's sake, what was I waiting for . . . a prince? Would it have been better? Is there anything that would have made all this better? It's all ripped away from me. All my dreams of a man who would love me . . . Who's going to love me now? I wish I'd had sex all those times when I . . . then I'd know how it was supposed to feel. Then I'd have something to remember. Now all I have is this.

I feel his body on top of mine as if he's here right now, right this moment. I feel so nauseous. I'm afraid I might throw up. Dr. Johnson said to do whatever was necessary not to throw up. I might choke, since I can't open my mouth wide enough. Thank you, I needed to know that. Knowing that I shouldn't . . . can't . . . makes it worse. My stomach is twisted into knots. I'm shaking like a leaf.

I never want to read this . . . ever. Just get it outside yourself, Teresa. Goddamn it, my face hurts. The throbbing is torturous . . . the pain unreal. If only I could sleep through this. There's a part of me that doesn't feel like me anymore. Maybe it's too soon.

I feel as if I'm in shock. It wasn't me in that house; it was someone he knew, or wanted to know. Or maybe someone he hated. I'm not sure how I mean it just yet, but I didn't feel like a person. When he kicked me low in the back as I lay on my side, I felt like an animal someone was kicking along the side of the road. It wasn't me he was hurting. It was someone, something, else. Because if it was me . . . then I really am nothing.

I'm cutting my hair off. All of it. I'd like to shave my head so that no one can grab me again. There were strange, strange things about him, about what he said to me. My heart is beating so fast, just thinking about him. I don't feel safe, not even here. But I'm sure there's no way he could be on this train. There's no way. He had to humiliate me, to degrade me. He reminded me of a small child who needs to have his own way. "You won't fuck me? Okay, I'll fuck you." He said it to me again and again. But I didn't understand, don't understand, what he meant. I hadn't talked back to him. I couldn't. My jaw was already broken. Who was he talking to? He knew that raping me would be the ultimate hurt. He made sure I'll never lose these bruises, not the ones on the inside. God . . . God . . . God . . . God . . . Please make it stay light outside. Why is the light slipping away?

The lady next to me was irritated that I kept getting up. "Can't you just sit still . . . dear?" The condescending "dear" on the end.

No, I want to say to her. Yell to her. No, I can't sit still. A man just raped me in his house for fourteen hours. For fourteen fucking hours! Do you know what that does to a person? Do you? Do you know what it does to feel someone's hand coming down on your throat and feel the room getting dark and think you're going to die any minute if he doesn't get off you? Do you? I want to scream at her, to make her cry. I want her to feel the pain I feel. And I'm ashamed of myself. To hell with her. How dare she tell me that I can't keep getting up. I just had fourteen hours of someone telling me I can't get up.

I can't say anything, though. Even if my mouth wasn't wired nearly shut, even if I didn't have the stitches in . . . I can't say anything. My voice is gone and I'm scared. What could she do to me if she was angry? Could she hurt me? I don't trust anyone. "Before" I might have talked to her . . . I probably would have had a nice conversation during the trip . . . but now? No. Just leave me alone.

I keep having to go to the restroom. I hate the walk back there; I feel like everyone is staring at me. That everyone knows what happened in that house. That everyone can see me with my clothes off and bloody. That everyone can see me lying on the mattress with my hands tied. Shaking. Scared to death. That everyone sees the huge, red "R" on my forehead. That no one cares. It hurts to go to the bathroom. It hurts to raise my skirt and lower my underpants. It hurts to sit down. It hurts to pee. Everything hurts. I'm still bleeding . . . this should stop. It can't be right to lose this much blood. How much would I have to lose to die? It feels like a lot, but maybe it's not that much. I can't do anything about it, anyway. Just don't think about it. Maybe he hurt me, though. Maybe he hurt me more than I realize. What did he put inside me? What did this guy do to me?

I feel so vulnerable. If anyone wanted to hurt me, all they'd have to do is hit me in the face. I'm afraid of falling. What if I fall on the way to the restroom and pull out my stitches? It could be forever before I get help . . . out here in the middle of nowhere.

Teresa . . . pull yourself together!! Just keep writing . . . it'll keep you sane. Stay sane. Writing. And food. They're the only things that calm me, and since I can't eat . . . Well, sex. I always imagined sex as calming, lying back in my lover's arms, satisfied . . . calmer than calm . . . serene, tranquil. Discovering the beauty of love.

I can't imagine ever wanting a man inside me again. Touching me. Opening my legs. Penetrating me. Coming inside me. I hate the way the men on the train are looking at me. I feel like they know. They know when they see a woman who's been raped. I can see it in their eyes. They want a piece. They're curious . . . did I enjoy it? Did I come? My heart is beating so loud. My ears are pounding. My breath . . . I can't catch my breath . . . I'm so scared.

The woman sitting next to me . . . she tells me her name is Maryanne . . . is trying a different approach. She's figuring that if she talks to me, I won't get up and down as often. Plus, she wants to sit on the inside, since I keep getting up. I feel panicky so far away from the window, but, as usual, I acquiesce. She's irritating me now. What she doesn't know is that she's making me feel more like I have to leave. Why do people always do this to me? Keep me where I don't want to be . . . talk to me. She's going home to Chicago (who cares?) and has three children (really, who cares?). I don't want to seem cold, I just . . . I'm tired and sleepy and I can't rest and I can't sleep. And I'm sore . . . all over sore.

She's interpreting my inability to talk as a sign of my wanting to listen. I feel so . . . snared by her. Tangled up in a web like a spider who can't move. She starts speaking to me like I'm a child. She had learned long ago, she tells me, to obey her husband . . . that a woman has her "womanly duties" that she must learn how to master . . . blah, blah, blah . . .

At first I just listened politely until it dawned on me that she was insulting me. She was insinuating that I'd done something to deserve what she perceived was a beating from my husband or boyfriend. I'm so pissed at myself. Why does it never dawn on me that people are trying to hurt me? Why am I never on guard? Why do I always let people hurt me?

I'm so tired of being judged. Rape. The ultimate judgment. The ultimate "fuck you." I try to be good. I've never hurt anyone. Why am I being punished?

I nodded every now and then as she talked. A couple of strategically placed "um huhs." She droned on and on. She was killing me. And I had another thirty hours on this train. God, take me now!

She started talking about where she was on Wednesday . . . then Thursday. I realized suddenly that she was talking about the same Thursday evening I was being raped. And brutalized. Two people. Two different Thursdays. She gave me details. Details no one asked for. I wanted to give her my details.

Let's see, Maryanne . . . in the afternoon I was dragged off the street by some bastard who thought it great sport to take me in his house and rape me. Details. Well, he wasn't too happy with me. So what he did was push me so hard that I hit my head on the floor and was knocked out for a while. He wasn't too happy with me hitting my head and blacking out and spoiling his fun, so he decided he was going to rape me. Only you know what, Maryanne? He couldn't get it up. The pig. So he decided that I needed to pay for his inadequacy. What I needed at that moment was a good beating. Let's see . . . how about . . . a broken jaw? Oh, and maybe . . . yeah, busted lower teeth . . . that'll take about forty-five stitches. Details. Here, Maryanne, let me give you more details . . .

Let's see, somewhere in there, a couple of times, he tried to penetrate me again but couldn't. He still wasn't hard enough. I wasn't in quite enough pain for him to get hard enough to get inside me and come. He told that I was even more beautiful when I was in pain and that he could get off on that big time. Do you know what that means, Maryanne? More pain. A lot more. He was even "thoughtful" enough to tell me how he was going to do it. How he was going to cut my nipples off. How he was going to rape me until I couldn't walk. And you know what I was doing while he was saying these things, Maryanne? I was concentrating really hard on not going insane. I was that scared. I concentrated on separate parts of him. On lines in his face. The color of his eyes. The curve of his lip. They were all just pieces of a person without any glue holding him together. I was trying to form a face in front of me. This was so surreal to me.

Details. The weak, ignorant, arrogant, useless excuse for a human being couldn't even do what animals can. And I wanted him to, Maryanne, because I knew if he couldn't, my chances of getting out of that house were very slim. Shit. I'm so angry. How dare he use me for a receptacle. How dare he do this to me. How dare he ruin my life with his viciousness.

I'm in deep trouble. I'm going to go mad sitting here listening to this woman.

It's 11:00 . . . the man behind me has his light on, reading. Must have dropped off. He looks like a nice older man, but I don't trust him being behind me. I don't want anyone behind me. I feel apprehensive, and when he moves, I imagine his hands coming down over my head, grasping me around the neck, his fingers encircling each other . . . squeezing. Tighter . . . tighter . . . until I can't breathe. Until all I see is black. Until I no longer exist. And no one notices. My chest is rising and falling. My sweater lays against the scarred skin on my chest. My heart is beating so loudly. I feel like everyone can hear. My breath comes in short pants. He's rustling behind me. All he did was reach up and turn off the light, though. This is really getting to me.

I didn't go back for dinner; I didn't want to walk back there with everyone watching, and anyway, what's the point? I'd only be able to suck on a soda. But I'm starving. I probably should get some kind of liquid drink like Citrocal — I think that's the name. I should look into that when I get to Daddy's. I doubt if I can get it on the train.

My mind is consumed with what happened. I hate the dark. My insides are so sore. Way up inside . . . deep. Deep inside my abdomen and up into my stomach. I'm afraid he's hurt me really bad. I hope it isn't permanent. What did he put inside me? It felt sharp, and some of the cuts I have on my hands, I think, are from it. What was "it"? Cold. Pushing it in and out until I was ready to scream, but when I moved my mouth, I felt my bones grinding, so I kept my voice inside. I tried to grab it from him, but my hands were tied and I couldn't grasp it. We struggled for awhile. My back was in spasms. The cramps were agonizing. I tried to stretch them out, but whatever was inside me hurt more. I was pushing it deeper inside with the twisting around I was doing.

I just wanted him to stop. My pain turned him on. I could feel it; I could feel him against my leg. It was hard. So sick. I don't remember very much of what happened. I can't think straight. I can't sleep. I'm a mess. And I'm scared. The night is longer than long on this damn train.

I woke again with a start. It was light out now. I didn't move for a moment. It's only been two and half days. Astounding how much has happened. It's hard to believe I'm going to my dad's funeral. So much has happened. Maryanne came back from breakfast this morning and started talking to me again. I was determined to be more myself. I'm sort of ashamed for being so insensitive toward her. My situation is not her fault.

She started talking to me, at me, again when I had an idea. I'd been writing in my notebook and thought it might be a good idea to write a note . . . tell her my name . . . explain that I had broken my jaw and couldn't talk. She read my note and nodded. I wanted to write her another note telling her that she could talk, that she didn't have to nod her answers, but I knew she wouldn't quite get my sense of humor. Or lack of it, at this point. Anyway, her manner changed. Like someone who was talking to a blind person, she talked louder! And she used more pronunciation in her words. I wanted to tell her . . . Maryanne, I can hear, I just can't talk, but . . . didn't. It was too much effort, so I sort of lay back against my chair and listened.

She told me about her daughter and new grandchild she had been visiting, and in all honesty, it sort of took my mind off things. I looked past her to the countryside rushing past us. We couldn't get there fast enough for me. In fact, a momentary thought of catching another train for New York crossed my mind for a moment. I just wanted to get there, go to the funeral, and go home. No, not home. I wanted to go . . . anywhere . . . nowhere . . . I just wanted to feel safe again. Part of me wanted to ride and ride forever . . . part of me wanted to get off this damn train . . . this rolling coffin.

Suddenly Maryanne made a move toward me, reaching for my hands laying on my lap. Panicked, I drew my hands back and looked into her eyes. I'm sure I frightened her as much as she did me. An animal sound came out of my mouth, louder than I had intended, I'm sure. I didn't want to be touched. Please . . . just . . . don't touch me.

"Dear . . . dear . . . you went somewhere, dear. Have you been listening to me? I think you may have . . . " She leaned toward me, whispering, " . . . started." Started what? My eyes were drawn to where her eyes were looking.

Blood had seeped through the back of my skirt and was working its way along the sides and between my legs, onto my seat. Shit. Shit. Shit. I resisted jumping up in my seat, afraid that others might see what had happened. "Ah . . . " was all I managed to get through my lips. I wrote furiously on my paper. "Could you please get my suitcase from the overhead?" She did, dropping it on my lap. I looked around in my suitcase for another skirt. It was wrinkled, but clean. The only other thing I had to change into was a pair of jeans, but I knew they would be uncomfortable.

I grabbed a sweatshirt and wrapped it around my waist, turned and placed another sweatshirt on my seat. I worked my way back to the restroom. It seemed like everyone was either coming or going to breakfast. I kept my head down and managed to whisper tiny "Excuse me's" as I snaked my way through people to the restroom. Christ.

I was bleeding all over the place. I cleaned up . . . how humiliating. But I had to tell someone. I was afraid if they thought I was sick or injured, they might make me get off the train for medical attention and I would get stuck . . . wherever we were.

I found the porter and wrote a note to him, pointing at my jaw, hoping he'd understand. "I have a broken jaw and have to write this out. I've had an accident and would appreciate it if you'd help me clean it up." How degrading. I couldn't talk to him, couldn't make small talk as I stood there waiting for him to finish. There I stood with a stranger cleaning up blood on my seat. People were watching. It seemed everyone came over to look at what was happening. How could it get worse than this? How embarrassing.

I wrote the porter a note as he finished, thanking him for his help. I didn't know what else to do. A strange thought crossed my mind . . . do I tip him for this? I really didn't know the proper etiquette in a case such as this.

As I sat back down, I knew I had to face the fact that the guy had hurt me much more than I thought. I have to get to a doctor as soon as I can. I don't know where I'm bleeding from.

Maryanne came back from . . . wherever. Probably lunch by this time. She left me when she saw what a mess I had on my seat. I could tell she was embarrassed. I don't blame her. I would have left too. Actually . . . no . . . I wouldn't have. I would have stayed with her.

I don't want anyone behind me. Ever. "You ever had it in the ass?" No, I wanted to scream in his face. I haven't "had" it anywhere. Nowhere but where you've put it so far. I went from crying, which made him angry . . . to sobbing, which made him angrier . . . to making some sort of scared animal sounds, which made him furious with me. I didn't want him to do this to me, not like this . . . anything but this. No one has ever hated me that much, to want to hurt me that badly.

He turned me over. No . . . No . . . I can't. I've never . . . I struggled against his body, but he was stronger than strong. At first I couldn't breathe. He crushed my face into the mattress, but my hands were still tied. Untie my hands, you ass . . . I have to breathe. You're going to be fucking a dead person if you don't untie my hands. You're going to be fucking a dead person! A dead person! Inside my head, I was bold and assertive . . . "Untie me!" In reality, my actions were timid . . . begging with him, as much as I could with my jaw broken . . . pleading for him to untie me so I could breathe. I was more than afraid, and tears were welling up in my eyes. More than horrified at the torture he could dream up. And I hate myself. Thinking about it now makes me nauseous, but it's inside me. I feel like throwing up everything inside me. I feel like he's still inside me.

He stuffed a cloth in my mouth. He jammed the dirty, bloody, disgusting cloth in my mouth. It was repulsive. Shaking . . . shaking . . . shaking . . . I can't stop. This is never going to end. Never going to be okay. Life is never going to be okay again. My hatred for this person is overwhelming. It's in my skin. In my bones. In my blood. Inside of me. The hatred is a part of me now. He's raping me over and over and over again. He's raping me right now in my mind. He's raping me right now . . . in my mind. I couldn't get any leverage . . . then he let my hands go. I held onto the mattress. I was on my hands and knees. At first I thought he was . . . going to . . . I thought at first he was going to . . . this is excruciating. I thought at first he was going to enter my vagina, but instead he . . . I can't do this. I have no one to talk to. I have to get this out of me. I remember looking down at my hands . . . they weren't mine anymore. They were disconnected from my body, cut and bloody. And I looked up and . . .

God . . . God . . . God . . . why did you leave me here by myself? Where did you go? I was standing in the corner looking at myself. I know I'm going crazy. I feel so . . . disconnected. I'm outside myself watching what's happening to me. Jesus. My hands are shaking . . . I want to die. So horrendous, these feelings. Why didn't he kill me? I can't live through this. My hip is so sore . . . the more I move, the sorer it becomes, so I just try to sit still. Impossible.

I try to calm myself. I don't want to wake Maryanne. I really don't want to wake Maryanne. The thought of him inside me is too much. I can feel his thighs against mine, holding onto my hips, pushing into me. And his voice. He's cruel and mean. He's going to make me feel like I want to die, he tells me. I do. I do already, just please don't do this to me. And he rears back and rams himself high into me one last time as he comes. He's deep inside me, ripping me, making me bleed. This is wrong . . . please . . . don't do this. The pain lifts me up, lifts my hands up off the floor, and they come back down with a thud. I lost my grip on the mattress. Jesus, I can't stand this. The pressure against my back is excruciating. I'm going to break in two. Why can't I sit still? Why does it hurt so much to sit?

I woke up sweating, and I have to write some more. Have to stay sane. Have to get to Michigan. I was deep in a nightmare, and I'm not sure if I said anything, or how loud I was if I did. But when I opened my eyes, there was a guy from a couple of seats in front of me, turned around, just staring. He frightened me. I looked around for my notebook and pencil, scared that someone had it . . . that someone took it while I slept, but I found it under my seat. I have to be more careful. This isn't something I want anyone to see.

It's still light, and I guess most people are in the dining car having supper. Maryanne is gone. The nightmare was horrible, but then I realized, it's what happened. What I can remember, anyway. There are whole chunks of time that I just . . . can't remember . . . I'm so scared. What if this means I'm going nuts? How am I ever going to be able to go to college? Who's ever going to love me? Who's ever going to want to make love with me?

I'm broken now. Too many questions. I drive myself nuts doing this. Always asking questions. *Always living inside my head. I'm so lonely. All I want is to talk to someone. Talk. To someone. But I have no one. I can't help crying, but at least not too many people are around. Just this stupid guy who keeps turning around. Don't look at me! Don't think about me! Don't do anything to me! He just stares into my eyes, and I avert mine. I can't play this game. Just leave me alone.*

I'm in the house again, even though it's the last place I want to be.

His voice was haunting me. I wished he would shut up. He kept telling me what he was going to do to me. His words, what he was going to do . . . the anticipation . . . was as bad as when he did it. Maybe worse. Part of me doesn't ever want to forget what he put me through; I never want this to happen to me . . . to anyone . . . again. He said he was going to slice my chest. My nipples. He was going to cut them off. I was so scared that he was planning to do it. He was high, but a different kind of high. He was on something that made him powerfully strong. I could tell when he grabbed me by the shoulders and pushed me. I went flying . . . flying across the room. I was afraid I was going to crack my head open when I hit the floor, but I just passed out.

Later he seemed to have taken something that was really strong, because he went into the kitchen and began talking to me differently than he had before. Music was coming in the windows from the staircase of the apartments behind his house. He started swaying back and forth; his mouth was moving to the words, but no sound was coming out. It felt strange. The room was eerily quiet. I felt as if I'd lost my hearing . . . just the music, low and in the background . . . no sounds coming from him . . . just his mouth moving. His eyes closed and his head rolled back.

I held my breath. Something in the moment made me feel really, really disturbed . . . like he was going to do something to me, something worse than what he had already done. All at once, he moved his head straight and then down over the counter to look at me, and he opened his eyes. They were darker than before, and cold. He was everything evil. "Have you ever been really hurt? I mean, really hurt?"

My first response " . . . *Yes, you fucker, I think I qualify right now, as a matter of fact . . .* " wouldn't have helped my situation. It was probably just as well that I couldn't talk. I might have made it more difficult on myself. I shook my head. I hadn't. Maybe he wouldn't hurt me any more because he felt bad for me . . . or maybe he would hurt me worse because he felt I deserved it. Everything came down to either/or . . . black/white . . . yes/no. 50/50. Those were my odds. I had a 50/50 chance of being tortured. Or not.

"Well, maybe it's about time . . . " He came through the kitchen door with a knife in *his hands. My eyes were wide and dry; I could feel it. My heart jumped into my throat. He could kill me now, and I wouldn't exist. At all. I couldn't think of what to do. My hands were still tied . . .*

I'm obsessed. Obsessed with thoughts of how <u>this</u> man arrived at <u>this</u> action at this moment in time. Did he lie on the mattress on which he raped me and think about the kind of girl he would pick? Did he think of how he was going to do it? Did he think of me and what it would do to me as he was planning it? Am I human any more?

I see the man before me and scream at him in my mind. "Who do you think you've picked to rape, you stupid son of a bitch? Someone important? Someone who has people who care for her? No, you've picked someone nobody gives a shit about. You've picked me, and I don't even care about me. You stupid son of a bitch. I deserve all that you're doing to me. Please don't let me live."

I'm losing my mind. I'm sure I'm losing my mind.

"God, this trip is taking forever." Maryanne was talking at me again.

I slipped into a nauseating grip of despair. Like a weary traveler along a narrow, steep path, I feel that at any moment I could slip and fall and it would be glorious because this would all be over. All would be black and calm. And over.

As she prattled on, I began my dialogue with her in my mind again. I just couldn't help myself. Want to know what forever is, Maryanne? Fourteen hours, Maryanne. Forever is in actuality fourteen hours with someone who is doing unspeakable things you've never even dreamt could happen. Forever is one hour . . . then two . . . then four . . . in an empty house with a strange man who wants only to hurt you. Forever is seeing time stretch in front of you with no ending. No idea of what is going to happen the next moment. Do you know what that's like, Maryanne? Do you? Do you know, Maryanne, how much you take for granted your next moment? How you think you have control over all your moments?

You don't. Forever is fourteen hours in a house with heavy tasseled shades and the smell of paint and . . . a noxious smell that makes you feel as if you're going to throw up any moment. Forever is lying on a musty, stained mattress and getting the smell in your skin and your hair and having your face pushed into the striped material until you choke. Fourteen hours in a house where a family might have lived only weeks before but is now your hell. A house in which you might die. That's forever, Maryanne . . . waiting to die. Having a gun shoved against your cheek. You know what it's like, Maryanne, to hear someone pull the trigger of a gun against your cheek? To hear the click of it in your ear?

To wait for the bullet to rip through your flesh, tear into your head, to feel the agony of your bones blowing apart? That's forever, Maryanne . . . waiting for all that . . . that's forever. Forever is how long I have to live with this.

I set the envelope down on my desk. Prior to meeting Gary, I ached to be out of that house. I wanted nothing more than to forget the image of seeing myself on a mattress, being raped.

But I realized that wasn't my reality. Even if I could have moved myself out of the house, it wouldn't make me free. I had to help myself through the fourteen hours I spent on the mattress in order to gain acceptance of my feelings, my thoughts, and particularly my actions on that day and others that followed. Only then could I comprehend the evil I went through and provide myself with compassion.

Chapter 21

November, 1997

"It wasn't a flashback . . . and it wasn't a nightmare."

I began almost before I sat down. I was agitated and confused and desperately needing Gary's help. Again. Which irritated me. Again. *When am I going to not need him?* I remember asking myself as I launched ahead.

"It was . . . a recollection. An intense memory. I'm back in the house. I can't believe I didn't recall all this until now. It was just a moment. A moment in the fourteen hours. When is this going to stop?" My eyes pleaded with him to help me as I told him what had happened . . .

It was Tuesday evening. It was an incredibly stressful time, both at work and with personal things, and I wasn't feeling well. I figured if I lay down for a couple of hours, maybe I could still do some work that evening. I pulled back the covers and lay down with my clothes on. Suddenly I was on the mattress, in the house. This hadn't happened in so long. At first I couldn't figure out what was going on.

I was inside myself. For so much of my time in the house, I felt as if I was outside myself, but I was in my skin now. I was on my back, lying on the mattress. I could smell it. Musty, horribly dirty. My knees were bent. My underwear and tights were off, and my jean skirt had only the first snap snapped. It must have been after he broke my jaw, because when I tried to talk, I couldn't move it. I could feel that my lip had swelled and tasted of blood. My blouse and skirt were open, and my hands were tied.

The man was on his knees and to my right. He had one hand inside me and something like a tool in the other, and we were struggling. I tried to get up on my left elbow and grab his sweater. I could feel the material between my fingers.

"You're ... hurting ... me ..." All I could manage was a whisper. He looked at me. He looked in my eyes. I remember them so clearly. The coldness. The lack of emotion. He brought his left hand back and brought it down hard against my left hip, puncturing my skin through my skirt. I remember thinking, realizing, saying to myself, "I don't matter."

I don't matter. It became my philosophy. It became my attitude, my claim, my belief, my position, my opinion. It became my doctrine, my sentiment. It became my conviction about myself. It became me.

The experience of reliving that moment, such a small moment during those fourteen hours, was an awareness I hadn't realized or had the privilege of knowing before that Tuesday. It was the naming of my suffering, those three small words.

And while it was intensely painful, Gary helped me realize it was a turning point for me. I had finally seen the monster in the closet and was astonished to learn that it was me.

I had to learn to treat myself gently because of my vulnerability, and tried to keep that in my mind as I looked at myself in the mirror that evening when I returned home. I had scars on my hands, my breast, my hip; my jaw and my teeth will never be the same. I lived through something no woman would want to live through, and gave birth to a baby who was stillborn. I can't have children because of the rape. I had emotional difficulties that I wouldn't want anyone to experience ... and still, *still*, I felt that I didn't matter. I didn't matter.

That I could reach this awareness was a miracle to me. The intense work of therapy that was necessary to reach this point was vital. Every moment of it. Every tear shed, every fear brought to light, every thought shared, every moment of it, was crucial. I had named my problem and could begin to comprehend and accept my decisions, my feelings, my actions, my behaviors.

As I stood looking in the mirror at the person I was that day, I felt overwhelming gratitude toward those in my life. My husband, my family, my friends. They accepted me with my scars, both inside and out. They loved me and cared for me and never once told me that I didn't matter.

● ● ●

About IIR

The Institute for Interpersonal Relations is located along Monterey Bay in Pacific Grove, California.

We are a small, independent publisher and seminar provider specializing in the mental health field, and concentrating on unique views of relationship issues not addressed elsewhere.

In addition, we try never to stray from the formidable goals of presenting the truth in difficult situations, and their consequences, and bringing our readers into the heart and minds of those who have experienced them.

Further, we are of the opinion that the expert is often the client in a therapeutic relationship, and can be a valued teacher who lives by the ideal that words bring comfort.

To request Teresa Lauer for speaking engagements, or to receive information on our seminars, please call, write, e-mail, or visit our website at the following:

Institute for Interpersonal Relations
612 Lighthouse Avenue, Suite 238
Pacific Grove, California 93950

E-mail: iirelate@ix.netcom.com
Website: www.irelate.com